STATE
POLITICS
and
ISLAM

State
Politics
and
Islam

Mumtaz Ahmad (ed)

American Trust Publications

Library of Congress
Catalog Card Number
85 - 073208

ISBN 0-89259-058-0

Printed in the United States of America
Typeset by NAIType

To Anwar H. Siddiqui
Zafar   Ishaq   Ansari
and   Qasim Murad
        in friendship

Say [O Muhammad]: "Unto whom belongs the earth and all that lives thereon.? [Tell me this] if you happen to know [the answer]!"

[And] they will reply: "Unto Allah."

Say: "Will you not then pay attention [to this]?"

Say: "Who is it that sustains the seven heavens and is enthroned in His awesome almightiness?"

[And] they will reply: "[All this power belongs] to Allah."

Say: Will you not then remain conscious of Him?"

Say: "In whose hand rests the mighty dominion over all things, and who is it that protects [all], but there is no protection against Him? [Tell me this] if you happen to know [the answer]!"

[And] they will reply: "[All this power belongs] to Allah."

Say: "How, then, can you be so deluded?"

We have conveyed to them the truth: and yet [look at them], they are intent on lying [to themselves]!

al-Mu'minūn: 84-90

CONTENTS

PREFACE

This volume is the result of an international seminar on "Islamic Political Thought and Institutions" held on September 6-8, 1982 at Purdue University, Indiana. The seminar was sponsored by the Association of Muslim Social Scientists (AMSS) and was attended by eminent scholars from the Muslim world and North America.

I wish to thank the then executive committee of the AMSS for allocating funds for the seminar and participants. I am especially grateful to Dr. A. W. Fakhri, Dr. Talat Sultan, Dr. Mushtaqur Rahman, and Mr. Dawood Zwink for their sustained moral encouragement and intellectual support at every stage of the preparation for the seminar. I must also extend my appreciation to Dr. Ya'qub Mirza who provided the administrative support and made physical arrangements for the seminar. Without his energy, good humor, and management skills, the seminar would not have been that successful. I am indebted to Prof. Hafeez Malik of Villanova University who helped arrange a travel grant for Prof. Sharif al-Mujahid's participation in the seminar through the American Institute of Pakistan studies.

The papers of Prof. Khurshid Ahmad and Dr. Muhammad al-Awa who took part in the seminar could not be included in the volume because the edited versions of their presentations were not made available in time. I wish to thank, however, both of these eminent scholars for their significant contributions during the seminar.

I am also grateful to Mr. Tariq Quraishi of the American Trust Publications without whose persistence and constant reminders this volume would never have been completed. Mr. Quraishi also helped in preparing the final manuscript with care, incisiveness, and sound guidance.

I hope this volume will contribute in some small measure toward a better understanding of the issues involved in the study of Islamic political theory. Needless to say, the views expressed in these papers are those of the individual authors and do not necessarily represent those of the AMSS.

Mumtaz Ahmad
Washington, D.C.
20 August 1986

NOTES ON CONTRIBUTORS

Mumtaz Ahmad has studied Political Science at the University of Karachi, American University of Beirut, and the University of Chicago. He has taught at the National Institute of Public Administration, Karachi, Pakistan. Besides being a consultant in Southwest Asian affairs in Washington, D.C., he is the associate editor of the *American Journal of Islamic Social Sciences*. His publications include *Bureaucracy and Political Development in Pakistan, The Kashmir Dispute*, and *Studies in Rural Development and Local Government in Pakistan*.

Khalid M. Ishaque is an attorney at law, Supreme Court of Pakistan. An eminent constitutional lawyer and a human rights activist, Mr. Ishaque is the author of a number of works on Islamic constitutional and legal theory. He has also served as advocate general of West Pakistan and a member of the Islamic Advisory Council of Pakistan.

Javed Iqbal holds doctorate in Philosophy from Cambridge University. He is the author of numerous works on Islam and Pakistan, including *The Ideology of Pakistan*. Until his recent promotion to the Supreme Court of Pakistan, he had been the chief justice of the Punjab High Court.

Fathi Osman holds Ph.D. in Islamic History from Princeton University and has taught at Riyadh, Princeton, Temple, and Imam Muhammad Ibn Sa'ud universities. He is currently the editor-in-chief of *Arabia: The Islamic World Review*. Publications include: *Origins of Islamic Political Thought; Islamic Political Thought: A Contemporary Vision; Islamic Legal Thought;* and *Islamic-Byzantine.*

Fazlur Rahman is the Harold H. Swift Distinguished Service Professor of Islamic Thought at the University of Chicago. He has previously taught at the University of Durham, U.K., and McGill University and has served as director of the Central Institute of Islamic Research, Pakistan. Publications include: *Islam; Islamic Methodology in History; The Philosophy of Mulla Sadra; Prophecy in Islam; Major Themes of the Qur'an;* and *Islam and Modernity.*

Ahmad Moussavi holds Ph.D. in Islamic Studies from McGill University. He has served in the diplomatic service of Iran before the revolution.

Abdulaziz A. Sachedina teaches at the University of Virginia, Charlottesville. He has published extensively on the shi'ite religious and political thought. He is the author of *Islamic Messianism: The Idea of Mehdi in Twelver Shi'ism.*

Jamilah Jitmoud obtained her Ph.D. in Islamic Studies from the Ball State University, Indiana.

ISLAMIC POLITICAL THEORY: CURRENT SCHOLARSHIP AND FUTURE PROSPECTS

Mumtaz Ahmad

The current debate on Islamic resurgence has brought issues relevant to the nature, characteristics, and scope of an Islamic state and a distinctly Islamic political system into sharp focus. Many publications with widely varying theoretical positions and ideological implications have appeared on the subject. Most of them, however, only report current political events in the contemporary Muslim world without making any attempt to deal with those aspects of political theory which could profoundly affect these events. Moreover, even their accounts of the current political scene remain superficial and unrelated to the tensions between the imperatives of continuity and the demands for change in the Muslim world.

The failure of the current literature dealing with Islam and politics to be both theoretically reflective and sensitive to the great and enduring questions underlying the normative basis and practice of government can largely be attributed to the inadequacy of the discipline itself. Modern political science has come to be so narrowly defined that it has lost touch with other aspects of the collective endeavors of human life. Using the metaphor of a "Temple of Science" for various human sciences, David Ricci has described political science as one of its columns.[1] If this metaphor is pursued further, it can be argued that this isolated column of modern political science has neither a foundation underneath nor a pediment overhead. A closer scrutiny of the current literature testifies to the fact that the theoretical foundations of contemporary political science are even more uncertain today than they were before the behavioral revolution. The rapid breakdown of old paradigms during the past three decades is a sufficient indicator of general crisis and intellectual ataxia in the discipline. The paradigms and theoretical frameworks traditionally used by political scientists seeking to understand and analyze Muslim world political dynamics – elite studies, developmentalism, group

---

[1]David M. Ricci, *The Tragedy of Political Science: Politics, Scholarship and Democracy* (New Haven: Yale University Press, 1984).

theory, authoritarianism, political culture, lego-constitutional and institutional analyses – are all being discarded by the discipline. The current emphasis on the political economy approach, revived in part by European neo-Marxism, has rendered many of the older works obsolete in terms of methodology and content.

It would be futile, therefore, to expect that any significant disciplinary progress – both in its normative bases and its systematic analyses – can be achieved by using existing theoretical models. It is imperative that we go beyond the traditionally restrictive parameters of individual social science displines in order to gain a more profound, holistic, and comprehensive view of man and society.

Both modern political science and practice exist within a conceptual framework whose philosophical assumptions, vocabulary, and methodology are primarily derived from concepts which evolved out of the European tradition. Insofar as the West has had a significant impact on the intellectual, socio-cultural and political ideas and practices of both Muslim and non-Muslim Third World societies, it is only logical to discuss their political conditions and prospects by employing the terminology of modern Western political discourse. However, it should also be kept in mind that there might be certain important and profound aspects of non-Western politics which might not fit into or be understood by the conceptual categories of Western political thought. One cannot, therefore, agree with Bernard Crick that even distinct forms of politics in the contemporary Third World cannot be "sensibly expressed in an alternative vocabulary,"[2] – that is, a vocabulary derived from non-Western intellectual sources. If Western political science is "a product with particular cultural roots,"[3] as Bernard Crick himself admits, it cannot possibly claim universal human relevance. As has been noted by many scholars, some of the most commonly used categories of political analysis are somehow changed and transformed when applied to societies and cultures in which they did not originate. This is not to say that comparative political research and analysis based on certain agreed upon and rigorously defined conceptual categories is not possible

---

[2]Bernard Crick,"On Theory and Practice," in *Theory and Politics* ed. Klaus Von Beyme (The Hague: Martinus Nijhoff, 1971), p. 276.

[3]Ibid., p. 277.

or desirable, but rather that modern political science is not adequately equipped to handle data from non-Western polities. In the view of contemporary Islamic political thinkers, for example, modern political science is deficient because it does not consider fundamental ethical questions.

A look at Muslim writers' contributions to, and articulation of, Islamic political theory is equally dismal. Most of the contemporary works produced by Muslim theorists fall into the category of "political doctrine," not those of "political theory" or "political philosophy." In both religious and political discourse, academic discussion has inclined either toward explicating classical and medieval jurisprudential texts or toward describing certain historically sanctified institutional structures of early Muslim polities. This tendency, in fact, both epitomizes and reproduces the present crisis in Islamic political thought. The failure of modern Muslim theorists to grapple with basic philosophical issues and their tendency to concentrate on the authentication of texts and the compilation of glossaries and historical trivialities has resulted in what has been described in a recent critique as "second-rate thought," "superficiality," and "incompetence."

Such an uncritical adoption of past theories and assumptions has tended to narrow down the range of those issues considered as pertinent to articulating a coherent set of political and social ideas. What is needed is a thorough reassessment of previous assumptions and conceptualizations of the political phenomenon. The primary reason for this is not that such ideas were erroneous at the time of their formulation, but rather that they have lagged far behind the changes witnessed in the last two hundred years and are therefore unable to provide relevant, realistic, and practical solutions to issues which did not exist when they were originally conceived.

The essays collected in this volume represent a serious attempt to reformulate Islamic political theory in the context of today's political realities and problems. They elaborate the theoretical substructure of Islamic political thought, identify its guiding principles, and examine how these principles were applied during different periods of Islamic history. They also seek to understand how classical, medieval and modern Muslim thinkers have formulated the guiding principles of Islamic polity and the various Islamic political systems which they produced. While critically analyzing some recent Islamic political experiments in Pakistan and Iran, these essays also indirectly examine the position and function of such modern-day political institutions as political parties, elections, parliaments, mass media, universal sufferage and so on in an Islamic political system.

The common theme running through all of these essays is that it is not the structure of the Islamic state which should constitute the focal point in constructing an Islamic political theory but its substructure and its goals. This is because the specific structural arrangements and features of one Islamic state may diverge from another due to differences in time and place, but their guiding principles and values must be those enunciated in the Qur'an and the Sunnah of the Prophet. The institution of *caliphate*, for example, is treated not as being eternally unchangeable, but as a concept and a goal that symbolizes the nature of political systems in Islam. As has been noted in a recent monograph on the Islamization of political science, any system, regardless of the structural form it must assume because of the requirements of time and space in which it exists, can be viewed as being in accordance with the caliphate system as long as it adheres to the fundamental Islamic principles for ordering the spiritual and secular affairs of the *ummah*.[4]

There is also general agreement among the contributing authors that democracy is the spirit of the Islamic governmental system, even though they reject its philosophical assumptions about the people's sovereignty. They believe that the majority's voice can constitute the basis for the legitimate exercise of political authority in an Islamic state only if it recognizes and remains within the perimeters of Allah's political and legal sovereignty. These authors argue that since the Qur'an commands Muslims to conduct their affairs through mutual consultation (shura) and grants the privilege of *khilāfāh* to the entire Muslim community rather than to a single individual or a specific group or class of people, the resulting shura and selection of a ruler must be based on the free will of the Muslim masses.

The volume begins with Mr. Khalid M. Ishaque's articles on "Problems of Islamic Political Theory." Mr. Ishaque points out a

---

[4]Abdulhamid Abu Sulayman, "Islamization of Knowledge with Special Reference to Political Science," *American Journal of Islamic Social Sciences* 2/2 (1985): 287-88.

number of methodological problems associated with the study of Islamic political theory, including the special methodology dealing with historical precedents and the resulting limits placed on our understanding of the Qur'an and the relevant Hadith literature. He also sets the tone for subsequent articles in his critique of the manner in which contemporary political issues facing Islamic societies are presented and handled. An underlying assumption, when faced with such situation, is that some non-Islamic institutions are intrinsically superior to and more effective than their Islamic counterparts, and that a way must be found to utilize them, even if it involves merely the renaming of those Western institutions. He maintains that most questions raised in contemporary discourse on Islamic political theory are loaded with a priori value judgments about the ethical superiority and political efficacy of Western political institutions when compared to those of Islam.

Mr. Ishaque argues that neutral questions about human problems encountered while governing society should be framed in universal terms, and that possible answers should be sought in different systems. By so doing, the enduring political questions could be examined in greater depth and on a wider scale, thus avoiding the handicap of considering historical forms as ethical imperatives. This methodology, according to Mr. Ishaque, is much more suited to comparative political research than the one based on merely reiterating the earlier texts. It is by such a reformulation that the political priorities of Islam could be properly established and significant differences and similarities with other systems determined.

For Justice Javed Iqbal, the central question of Islamic political theory is the establishment of an Islamic state based on the twofold concept of *fālah* (happiness) – that is, it must establish institutional means for the success of the Muslim community in this world as well as prepare it for success in the hereafter. As a point of departure, Justice Iqbal begins by analyzing the political and constitutional implications of the three main features of an Islamic state: the supremacy of the *shari'ah*, the unity and the solidarity of the ummah, and the governing institution of the community (*khilāfah*).

As is well known, traditional Islamic political theory has been primarily concerned with the purpose of political authority – that is, the preservation and implementation of the *shari'ah* and the institution of political authority such as the selection of a caliph (*khalīfah, emīr, or imām*). While there has been a general consensus on the first point, opinions have differed sharply over who should be the caliph and what procedural formalities are required for his selection. There have also been substantial differences over the exact nature, scope, and extent of the caliph's authority in legislation, adjudication of conflicts and resolution of disputes pertaining to both religious and secular affairs. The state set up in Medinah by the Prophet cannot provide solutions to such problems faced today, for the Prophet's authority was derived from his status of being the messenger of Allah, meaning that his word could not be challenged. On the other hand, none of his successors, who were only political and administrative heads of the Muslim community, could legitimately claim absolute authority á la Prophet. Abu Bakr, upon his election as the first successor of the Prophet, clearly defined the limits of his role and authority as the head of the Islamic state by declaring:

> I have been made a ruler over you, though I am not the best among you. Help me if I am right; correct me if I am wrong. The weak among you will be strong with me until I have obtained for him his due, if Allah so wills; and the strong one among you will be weak with me until I have made him give what he owes, if Allah wills ... Obey me as long as I obey Allah and His Prophet; if I do not obey them, you owe me no obedience.[5]

However, with the transformation of the office of khilāfah into hereditary kingships during the Ummayyad and the Abbassid periods, and with the fragmentation of *dar al-Islam* into separate principalities, a different set of criteria came into being. Developed by the rulers and the political theorists, it retained the fiction of Abu Bakr's formulation while adding many loophole and exceptions in an attempt to redefine the relationship of the ruler to the ruled in the face of emerging political realities. A representative work of this period is *al-ahkām as-Sultānīyyah* by al-Mawardi, in which the foundation of the dominant Islamic political paradigm was laid out and remained undisputed until the emergence of the constitutional movement under Jamal ad-Din al-Afghani in the late nineteenth century. The only exception was

---

[5]Quoted by Abul A'la Maududi, "Political Thought in Early Islam," in *A History of Muslim Philosophy* ed. M.M. Sharif, vol. 1 (Wiesbaden: Otto Harrassowitz, 1963), p. 662.

the parallel evolution of shi'ite political theory, which rejected the idea of *ijma'* (consensus of the community) and sought to combine religious and secular authority in the person a semi-prophetic imām.

Justice Iqbal reassesses the significance of these questions for the contemporary Muslim world in the light of the Qur'an and Sunnah, and reinterprets the requirements of legitimate power within the framework of modern constitutional theory and practice. It is in this context that he discusses in detail the relevance of the separation of power between the executive, legislative, and judicial branches of an Islamic state as well as the built-in mechanism of checks and balances needed to ensure an institutionalized system of mutual accountability.[6]

Dr. Fathi Osman focuses on the modalities involved in appointing the head of an Islamic state as presented by both early historical practice as well as juristic formulations which evolved in the Islamic middle ages. Dr. Osman discusses the nature and scope of *bai'ah* (oath of allegiance) and its evolution from the days of the first four caliphs up until the era of the sultanate and multiple caliphates. Dr. Osman analyzes the chain of events which resulted in the painful transition from the actual implementation and use of bai'ah to its eventual reduction to a mere fiction.

Bai'ah has often been compared with the social contract theory elaborated in the seventeenth and eighteenth centuries by John Locke (d. 1704) and Jean-Jacques Rousseau (d. 1778). This particular theory assumes a mythical covenant made at an early stage of human history between the ruler of a given society and its people. This covenant stipulated that the leader, in his exercise of authority, is bound by the terms of the original social contract which put him in power. In the history of Islam, however, a real — not merely hypothetical — contract was drawn between the rulers and the ruled in the very first days of Islam. After the death of the Prophet in 11 A.H. / 632 C.E., the first four caliphs held their position as a result of a free public selection by the leading personalities of the day who truly represented the ummah. However, it was the people's public agreement and not the process

---

[6]A recent formulation goes even further and argues for the complete autonomy and separation of *al-Imāmah* (rulership), *al-Wizarah* (administration), *al-Qadha* (judiciary), and *al-Ifta* (legislature). See, Isma'il R. al-Faruqi, "Notes on the Islamization of Political Science "Unpublished), February 1985, pp. 4-6.

of selection which legitimized the caliph's rule over the ummah. This public agreement, called bai'ah, was inspired by the Qur'anic priciple of *shura* (mutual consultation). Dr. Osman traces the practice of *bai'at al imām* from its inception during the early caliphate when the office of the caliph was a truly elective one to its subsequent degeneration during the Umayyads and 'Abbassids to a body of electors consisting of only one person in order to ensure that a ruler could appoint his successor. Dr. Osman also shows how certain jurists tried to reconcile theory with actual practice when the Muslim world was becoming increasingly dominated by military dynasties. Most of the jurists, Dr. Osman argues, were more inclined to formulate rationalizations for the existing political realities than to uphold the purity of the ideal. As realists and pragmatists, their primary concern was to deal with the reality of the *al-Mutaghālibīn* (rulers who had imposed themselves on the community through the sheer power of their military might), while maintaining the legal fiction that legitimate power depends on the will of the community. Such being the case, the procedural as well as substantial requirements of exactly what constituted legitimate power were redefined with so many loopholes and exceptions that the original theoretical structure composed of universal participation, consensus, and mutual consultation simply collapsed. From then onward, Muslims were advised by their legal scholars to obey whoever was in power. The resulting disillusionment and cynicism is nowhere more evident than in al-Ghazzali's following passage:

> The concessions made by us are not spontaneous, but necessity makes lawful what is forbidden. We know it is not allowed to feed on a dead animal; still, it would be worse to die of hunger. Of those who contend that the caliphate is dead forever and irreplaceable, we would like to ask: "Which is to be preferred, anarchy and the stoppage of social life for lack of a properly constituted authority, or acknowledgment of the existing power, whatever it be? Of these two alternatives, the jurist cannot but choose the latter.[7]

This does not mean, however, that the imperatives of "al-'amr

---

[7]Quoted by D. de Santillana in *The Legacy of Islam*, ed. Sir Thomas W. Arnold and A. Guillaume (Oxford: 1931), p. 302.

bil-ma'ruf wal-nahy 'an al-munkar" (commanding what is good and forbidding what is evil) were ignored by all Islamic scholars. As Dr. Osman indicates in his well-structured article, some theologians and jurists did endeavor to restore the sanctity of the ideal, thus keeping the dream alive.

The debate as to whether Islam allows autocratic / monarchical rule as well as rule through some form of elective government was revived with a great deal of intensity during the constitutional movement in Turkey in the latter half of the nineteenth century. Most modern Muslim thinkers have maintained that since the Qur'an commands Muslims to conduct their affairs through shura or mutual consultation, the rule of autocratic kings is not allowed, and that a constitutional and representative form of government either with or without a king, is the only type of government permissible. A minority view, on the other hand, has proposed that since the common Muslim is almost totally ignorant of Islam and its values, he cannot realistically be expected to choose the right person to represent him. The interpretation of "mutual consultation" which this group finds acceptable and Islamically workable is that the head of state must appoint a shura council to advise him, with the understanding that their recommendations are not legally binding. A representative articulation of this postition was made by Maulana Mufti Mohammad Shaf'i, who claims that the ruler is entitled to select his own shura and that it does not necessarily have to be elected by the people.[8] According to him, the majority's opinion is, in most cases, "misguided" and "harmful." The ruler should, therefore, only use shura as a means to "enlighten himself on various aspects of the issue."[9] Thus, once he has consulted the shura, the ruler is free to do as he pleases.[10]

The two recent examples of this logic have been provided by President Zia-ul-Haq's nominated *majlis-i shura* in Pakistan and the institutionalization of the concept of the *vilayat-i Faqih* in Iran.

Professor Fazlur Rahman, in his thought-provoking contribution to this volume, critically examines the arguments advanced

---

[8]Maulana Mufti Mohammad Shafi', *Islam main mushawarat ki ahmiyat* [The Importance of Consultation in Islam] (Lahore: Adara-e- Islamiyat, 1976), p. 122.

[9]Ibid., pp. 128-130, 141, 172-74.

[10]Ibid., p. 176.

by these two contending points of view and maintains that the question of shura's role is integrally related to the concept of a ruler's power and authority in the Islamic contest.

More importantly, this debate raises the question of the role of the Muslim masses in an Islamic state and society. It would appear, Prof. Fazlur Rahman argues, that the foremost issue to be settled is that of the nature and function of the Muslim community. Can a situation be called acceptably Islamic, he asks, if the Muslim masses are so uninformed that they cannot be trusted with the task of choosing the right representatives to rule them; and, can an "all-wise" leader or a class of "religious experts" assume the governance of their affairs on their behalf while they themselves are "deaf, dumb and blind," to use a standard Qur'anic phrase?

Prof. Fazlur Rahman's analytic perspectives on the Islamically valid form of government, and how it is related to the Muslim community's duty to bear witness to the truth to mankind, are further elaborated in the context of shi'ite political thought as presented by Dr. Ahmad Moussavi. The problem Dr. Moussavi discusses here is the development of the theory of Jurist's Governance (vilāyat-i faqih), which has contributed to the formation of a body of twelver shi'ite 'ulema, namely the *marja'-i taqlīd* (locus of mass following), in Iran. While both vilayat-i faqih and marja'-i taqlīd are important subdevelopments of the imamate doctrine in shi'ite Islam, very few sunni Muslims are familiar with them. Dr. Moussavi examines the historical roots of these two concepts and situates them within the overall framework of shi'ite eschatology and political theory.

As enunciated by Ayatollah Khomeini, the concept of vilayat-i faqih is intertwined with such basic concepts of shi'ite religio-political thought as allegiance, imamate, and following (taqlid). According to this formulation, Islamic leadership is crystalized and embodied in the imamate, and is represented by God's infallible apostles and imams, whom all Muslims must obey. Imam Khomeini further maintains that during Imam Mehdi's occultation, imamate is continued by the leadership (vilāyat) of qualified jurists (mujtāhid and faqihs). A mujtahid or faqih thus possesses the right to govern as the representative of the infallible imam. In both religious and sociopolitical affairs, the relations of the people with the mujtahid are defined by the concept of taqlid – that is, following the incumbent faqih as if one were actually following the infallibe imam.[11]

Imam Khomeini's ideas on vilāyat-i faqih have provoked lively debate among both shi'ite and sunni scholars. Critics have contended that historically speaking, the concept of vilayat-i faqih represents a substantial deviation from mainstream sunni political theory and, so far as twelver shi'ism is concerned, an extraordinary innovation, for shi'ite imams have eschewed the acquisition of political power since the days of Imam Ja'far as-Sadiq.

Dr. Moussavi, on the other hand, argues that the process which culminated in the actualization of a supreme mujtahid or faqih ruling as the imam's deputy has a religio-historical background in post-Safavvid Iran. According to Dr. Moussavi, it was the establishment of the *usūlī* position through Aqa Baqir Bihbihani (d. 1784 C.E.) that laid the juridical foundations for the imam's deputyship. The victory of the usūlī ulema over the *akhbārī* not only led to the formation of the marja'-i taqlīd, but helped Mulla Ahmad Naraqi (d. 1824 C.E.) formulate the theory of jurist's governance in its general context. The theory of vilayat-i faqih, Dr. Moussavi states, is in some respects the continuation of the imamate doctrine since it was expected to govern the society during the imam's absence. The only difference between the two is that while deputyship is based on the rational choice of the people, the imamate derives its religiopolitical authority from the belief that the imam has been appointed to that office by God. However, the main factor of the individual rule of a charismatic leader remains the same in both conepts. Also, both imamate and deputyship are concepts which are primarily intended to provide moral legitimacy for the problems of power and governance in shi'ite Islam. In fact, they exemplify the way in which Islam seeks to unite religion and political power in a single institutional nexus. They are also intended to actualize the Qur'anic values of *'adl* (justice) and *qist* (equity) in the individual and social aspects of human behavior. Dr. Moussavi believes that in examining the position of the 'ulema and the shi'ite doctrine of marja'-i taqlīd, it is the notion of justice as enunciated in the Qur'an and Sunnah which must constitute the ultimate criterion.

The desire to create a just social order in Islam is not merely a narrow political goal; it is integrally linked with its soteriology

---

[11]Ayatollah Rouhollah Khomeini, *Tafsil ul-Shari'ah*, vol. 1 (Tehran: n.p.), p. 43.

because the central aim of Islam is to create the kingdom of God on earth. Dr. 'Abdulaziz Sachedina's paper explores this linkage with reference to both sunni and shi'ite political theory. This paper sets out with a discussion of Islamic soteriology which both created the historical reponsibility of establishing the ideal just social order and gave rise to an Islamic messianism, to be interpreted as the particular notion behind the creation of such a just social order within Islam. The function of the "Islamic messiah," the Mehdi, is to make justice triumph on earth. Thus construed, the idea of a messianic leadership which can fulfil this reponsibility is the outgrawth of the historical inability of the Muslim community to recreate the implementation of the Islamic ideas of justice after the end of the early caliphate (after the reign of 'Ali).

Dr. Sachedina categorizes the Islamic concept of justice as (a) positive-objective and (b) theistic. In his discussion of the Qur'anic conccepts of "universal" and "particular" guidance, he states that Islamic justice, although essentially theistic, recognizes elements of postive justice as a valid standard for the creation of a just order. It is in the "realm of universal objective justice that human beings are treated equally and held equally responsible for responding to the universal guidance" provided in the revealed text. However, unlike the natural law scholars of the Aristotelian tradition who were concerned with the relation of justice to society, Muslim jurists have traditionally discussed the concept of justice in relation to God's Will and have linked it to the role of man in this world and his destiny in the hereafter. Viewed from this perspective, "divine justice" becomes the ultimate objective of the Islamic revelation and is expressed in the sacred laws of Islam which deal with man's religious and secular affairs.

These sacred laws, embodied in the shari'ah and based on the twin sources of the Qur'an and the Prophet's Sunnah, are regarded as expressions of God's Will (and indicative of the 'way' by virtue of which divine justice is realized in history.) Thus, only the shari'ah can claim a legitimate basis of political authority. With the Qur'an and Sunnah of the Prophet forming "the constitutional instruments" and the "proximate" sources of authority in an Islamic polity, Dr. Sachedina argues that all personal interests and group preferences therefore become irrelevant. All claims to political power and authority must seek legitimacy on the basis of their conformity to shari'ah norms and principles.

While emphasizing the fundamental agreement of the sunni

and shi'ite jurists on the sources and objectives of divine justice as enshrined in the shari'ah, Dr. Sachedina also identifies their differences over the best way to make these ideals the dominant reality on earth. Along with Dr. Moussavi's paper on vilayat-i faqih, Dr. Sachedina's elaboration on some of the most important features of shi'ite political theory, especially the centrality of a messianic imam descended from the Prophet, who would reestablish the rule of justice and equity on earth, is an important contribution toward our understanding of the current religio-political debate in Iran.

Jamila Jitmoud examines the principles and guidelines of *jihad* as delineated in the Qur'an and the sayings of the Prophet. The study addresses itself to some of the most relevant questions of Islamic international law in its interactions with the contemporary world. Jitmoud's article becomes especially significant in view of this concept's misuse by the Western media[12] and scholarship and its frequent use by contenders in the now six-year-old Iran-Iraq war. Based on a unified presentation of primary sources, the study makes an important contribution to the theory of international relations in Islam.

Barring a few exceptions, the theory of international relations has been one of the most neglected fields of research among Muslim political thinkers.[13] This lack of scholarly interest among Muslim thinkers in issues pertaining to international relations is especially surprising in view of such modern developments as the abolition of the caliphate, the emergence of nation-states, and the establishment of international organizations. A theory of Islamic international relations capable of coming to terms with these changes and the challenge they pose to such traditional formu-

---

[12]A recent (August 1, 1986) *Washington Times* story by Martin Sieff on the Arab-Israeli conflict describes, of all the Arab rulers, Hafiz Assad of Syria as "obsessed" with the "Islamic cults" of "Jihad" and "Shahadah"!

[13]An earlier work in the field is Abul A'la Maududi's *Al-Jihad fil Islam* (Lahore: n.d.). A pioneering and non-apologetic presentation of the concept and practice of *Jihad*, Maududi's study examines the issues of war and peace in a historical-comparative perspective and makes a clear distinction between *Jihad* and the wars waged for worldly gains by Muslim rulers.

Another thoroughly researched and theoretically informed study on the subject is *The Islamic Theory of International Relations: Its Relevance, Past, and Present* by Abdulhamid Abu Sulayman, (Herndon, VA.: International Institute of Islamic Thought, 1987).

lations as *khilāfah, dar al-Islam, dar al-'Ahd,* and *dar-al-Harb* has yet to be formulated. The structure of international relations as constituted today, and the complex field of contemporary regional, pan-Islamic and global conflicts and alliances cannot be understood by referring to formulations propounded by classical and medieval Muslim thinkers.

This brings us to our concluding observations on what should be the priorities in future research on Islamic political theory. Although a considerable amount of theoretical literature has been produced during the last five decades on such subjects as Islamic constitutional theory; the nature of the caliphate; the concept of an Islamic state and its institutional structures; the Islamic form(s) of government; and the relationship of Islam with nationalism, democracy, and socialism; a number of subjects of decisive importance for Islamic political theory – especially as it relates to contemporary political dynamics – remain unexplored.

One does not find, for example, any sustained discussion on the interrelationship between political and economic systems.[14] Considering the fact that most demands placed on political system and public policy decisions emanating from the authoritative structures of the state have to take economic matters into account, absence of any extended discussion on this subject is a serious flaw in the current literature on Islam and politics. Much of the discussion on Islamic politics treats the economic environment as if it were largely irrelevant. As a matter of fact, the formal apparatus of contemporary Islamic political theory is heavily biased toward the assumption that the economic and political organizations of a given society will remain static. Furthermore, the economic sector is often perceived as only a passive recipient of policy outputs, not as an important factor in determining how a

---

[14]The only exception is an article "The Political Context of Islamic Economics: High and Low Road Strategies" by Ijaz Shafi Gilani in *Studies in Islamic Economics* ed. Khurshid Ahmad (Leicester, England: Islamic Foundation, 1980). pp. 131-142, where the author differentiates between goal-oriented and value-oriented political leaderships in Muslim societies and relates them to specific economic strategies (high and low) which are pursued in a given context. Dr. Javed Akbar Ansari also shows awareness of the interrelationship between politics and economics when he assesses the economic performance of the revolutionary Islamic government in Iran with reference to a set of value premises derived from its socio-political philosophy. See his article, "The Political Economy of the Islamic Republic" in *Arabia: The Islamic World Review* (July 1983), 22-24.

system operates. If politics means the acquisition and management of power, it logically follows that political theory must deal with the politicians' ability to affect, mobilize, and appropriate all kinds of power, including control over and use of such resources as land, factories, welfare, jobs, organizations, technology, goods and services, and media and expertise.

Another important area thus far neglected by Islamic political theorists is the role of administrative and bureaucratic structures in the political process. One can identify at least three closely related gaps in the current Islamic literature on this subject. First of all, no theorist has attempted to formulate a theory of administration separate from the general theory of politics. Second, and akin to this, is the general lack of awareness that policy issues pertaining to the internal structures of governmental organizations (i.e., level of intitutionalization, chain of command and hierarchical arrangement, authority structures, personnel recruitment, training and motivation, and nature, processes, and quality of decision making) are just as important for the Islamicity and efficacy of the state apparatus as are those concerns pertaining to the election of an emir or a shura. Since these questions are usually perceived as being purely technical problems, they are not deemed worthy of treatment at a broader conceptual level. Finally, by relegating issues *about* and *within* the administrative structures of the state to a trivial postion of "nuts-and-bolts" questions, Islamic political theorists have failed to recognize the intergral relationship between the processes of policy formulation on the one hand and policy implementation on the other. The conceptual and methodological assumptions underlying this failure were among the major factors responsible for the considerable gap between policy *outputs* and policy *outcomes* in the processes of Islamization in Pakistan during the Zia regime. The Islamists seemed to have assumed that a change in political personnel alone would be sufficient to bring about the Islamization of Pakistani society, and that existing administrative structures were value-neutral, represented no special interests except those of the present incumbents, and did not constitute an obstacle to programs implemented to change the society.[15]

---

[15]For an extended discussion of this see Mumtaz Ahmad, "Islamic Revival in Pakistan" in *Islam in the Contemporary World* ed. Cyriac K. Pullapilly, (Notre Dame: Cross Roads Press, 1980), pp. 261-271.

We believe that an original contribution can be made in the field of organization and bureaucratic theory with reference to Islamic perspectives on major problem areas in the field. Such research should be undertaken at four levels: 1) normative, 2) historical, 3) critical, and 4) empirical-prescriptive.

1) Normative. This will involve an elaboration and elucidation of the normative theory of administrative/managerial behavior as enunciated in the Qur'an and Sunnah. An attempt should be made to point out direct references in the Qur'an and Hadith literature explaining how administrative affairs *should* be conducted as well as deriving implications for administrative behavior from these sources. It is also worth noting that even though they do not directly address themselves to administrative behavior problems, they nevertheless are relevant to the moral and ethical principles of managing worldly affairs and governing interactions in various social situations. Such an undertaking will require a thorough study of the Qur'an and Hadith literature and a capacity to formulate an integrated theory of management and administration based on the relevant data collected. The resulting theory then has to be situated within the broader framework of the Islamic theory of state, society, and economy.

2) Historical. The historical approach will involve the description, analysis, and examination of administrative structures, institutions, and processes developed by various Muslim governments separated from each other by time and location. Such a study ideally would include 1) the administration of the State of Medinah under the Prophet, upon whom be peace; 2) the administration during the caliphate of the four rightly guided caliphs; 3) the administration of the Umayyads; 4) the administration of the 'Abbassids; 5) the administration during the Ottoman Caliphate; and 6) the administration during the Muslim rule in India, with particular reference to the sultanate and Moghul administration.

This historical survey will study the following aspects of administration:

a. Administration of the central government: its organization, structures of authority, and processes; institutionalization of shura and structural differentiation of power and functions.

b. Administration of the provinces and local areas.

c. Judicial administration: processes and procedures of adjudication and conflict resolution under the shari'ah; the nature of the court system, its personnel structures, and its relationships with executive authorities.

d. Financial administration: systems and structures of taxation, agrarian structures, with special reference to revenue administration; collection, distribution, and management of *zakah*.

e. Military administration: recruitment, training, and organization, and its relationship with civilian political authorities.

f. The structure of the civil services: recruitment authority patterns, and career conditions.

g. The nature of the relationship between state officials and the community, with special reference given to institutional structures for grievance handling — the institutions of *mazalem* courts and *muhtasib*;

h. The nature, extent, scope, and practices of public and private business enterprises and partnerships.

The preceding aspects of the administrative systems developed at various times and places by Muslim governments will be studied with reference to the following questions:

a. How much of the structure and processes of the administrative system and the *actual* behavior of Muslim administrators and managers was in line with the normative theory of the administrative system and behavior as outlined in the Qur'an and Sunnah?

b. Concerning the extent to which there was a significant discrepancy between *theory* and *practice* – what were the intervening variables in terms of the goals and orientations of the regimes, socio-economic and political expediencies, and local and external influences which created this gap?

c. With demarcation between areas of unity and diversity within these historical structures and processes also being crucial, can certain unifying characteristics and common guiding principles which underlie the apparently diverse structures and processes of both historical and contemporary Muslim administrative systems be identified?

3. Critical. At this stage a critique of modern organization and management theories — both normative as well as empirical — in light of the Islamic theory of administrative behavior and practice should be undertaken. This should involve an examination and critique of the folowing major modern theories:

1. The Marxist theory — considering the state as an "executive committee" of the dominant economic classes and private man-

agement as a system of expropriation of the surplus value created by labor.

2. The Weberian theory — with its emphasis on legal-rational bureaucratic structures as a prerequisite for efficient management.

3. The scientific management school — its "machine" model of man and its emphasis on productivity, efficiency, and "one best way" of doing things.

4. The human relations school — its assumptions regarding needs, motivation, and incentives.

5. The decision-making and other behvioral theories — maximizing/satisfying utility function.

6. The structural-functional approach.

7. The non-Marxist conflict theories developed by Collins, Crosier, Coser and Daherndorf.

This should also involve a critical study and evaluation of the management decision-making techniques and tools — PBPS, PERT, MBO, CPA, and so on — with special reference to their claim of being value-neutral, and the feasibility of their adoption by Islamic administration and management.

4. Empirical-Prescriptive. A critical examination and evaluation of the administrative management systems of contemporary Muslim states in terms of their structures and economic and business decision-making processes as well as the behavior patterns of their administrators and managers is another area which should warrant the attention of Muslim political theorists. This should be done with reference to the following objectives:

a. Building up and managing a true Islamic society.

b. Initiating, managing, and directing policies and programs of social, economic and political development within an egalitarian Islamic framework.

c. Creating new institutions or adapting existing ones until they are compatible with the teachings of Islam.

Another important issue which requires serious study lies in the respective roles of the public and private sectors in contemporary Muslim countries. This question needs to be studied in light of its ideological underpinnings, the respective stages of socio-economic and political development of various Muslim countries, welfare and egalitarian goals of the Islamic state, efficient utilization and management of natural resources, and the relative autonomy of the economy and society.

Parallel with these issues comes the study of policy formation and its processes in an Islamic political context. This area is one of the most important interdisciplinary subjects currently studied in social sciences. Precisely because the process itself is so complex and encompasses dynamic social actions and their effects upon society, it has been resistant to both adequate conceptualization and research. Theoretical models as well as empirically-oriented research projects in the field of policy analysis have long sought a set of organizing principles to better understand the process of policy formation and also to develop solutions to problems arising out of what was supposed to happen with what really did happen, and why it turned out contrary to the original intention of the policy makers.

The two competing paradigms of policy making — the rational actor model and the incremental model — both perceive the policy process as mainly static behavioral design. They also fail to synthesize organizational and political perspectives and to create a much-needed broader conceptualization of policy studies which is able to contend with questions of *values* as well as the *means* to realize those values in practice. An alternative model based on the Islamic perpective would, however, include an analytic discussion and a moral critique of *goals, means,* and *consequences*. This is what some modern Muslim thinkers (e.g., Abul A'la Maududi) have called research conducted not in terms of methods only but also of outlook.[16] These issues are important in sofar as descriptive theoretical generalizations about the way human beings make decisions inevitably assume a normative character and a value imperative – that is, once people follow the implications of descriptive generalizations, they become normative and self-fulfilling prophecies. It is, therefore, important that Muslim political scientists should strive to develop an alternative, Islamic theoretical perspective in the field of policy studies which supplemets research on (1) how man actually behaves with (2) how man ought to behave, and (3) how man's potentialities and capabilities can be liberated for fuller realization. In this way, Muslim plitical scientists can make a significant contribution toward enhancing our understanding of the relationship between

---

[16]Abul A'la Maududi, "Islami Tahqeeq" [Islamic Research], inaugural address at the Islamic Research Academy, Karachi, Pakistan, 1963.

political values. Questions of human freedom and institutional forms of social justice in policy making situations are not without religious and metaphysical contexts; yet, they are political and empirical enough to constitute a legitimate object of study by political scientists.[17]

Another area which has been largely neglected by Muslim scholars is the theory of political development and change. Most of contemporary writings on an Islamic state deal with an ideal and stable political system which is assumed to be in a perfect state of equilibrium. There is no discussion concerning a transitional period in the process of change from the present form of the state to its ideal aspect, and there seems to be no awareness that social and existential determinants of change will still operate even after the establishment of an ideal Islamic state. Muslim political theorists have concentrated mainly on criticizing the once fashionable theories of political development and change used by American modernization theorists during the 1950s and 1960s to analyse Muslim societies. One such modernization theory which has become a popular target of critique on the part of Muslim theorists is Daniel Lerner's *The Passing of Traditional Society*,[18] in which he maintains that as traditional Middle Eastern societies undergo industrializations, urbanization, media participation, and political involvement, they will internalize modern Western cultural values and norms and consequently abandon their traditional cultures. "What America is, ... [the] modernizing Middle East seeks to become."

Development, according to this formulation, is synonymous with Westernization. Traditional societies are seen as blocks of sand that would disintegrate upon contact with the West. Closely associated with this notion was the belief that the Western model of development was universally applicable – that is, development in Muslim societies would follow the general model of change in the historical West if and when they decided to modernize. Also associated with this was the prediction that industrialization, urbanization, and media expansion in these societies would inevitably lead to secularization and a consequent marginalization of

---

[17]N. Kokosalakis, "Theoretical Problems in the Human Sciences and the Systematic Study of Religion," *Changement Social et Religion* (Paris: C.I.S.R., 1975), p. 446.

[18]Daniel Lerner, *The Passing of Traditional Societies (New York: The Free Press, 1958)*.

religion in public life.

Recent changes in Iran and elsewhere in the Muslim world have shown that modernization does not necesserly bring about secularization and other characteristics of a Western industrialized/modernized society, and that more information is needed to better understand the nature and processes of political change in Muslim societies. One must also point out, however, that the Islamists who became the unintended beneficiaries of the wrong assumptions of modernization theorists were equally erroneous in their analyses of the nature of change in Muslim societies. While modernization theorists were so preoccupied with the impact of secularism that they neglected the resilience of Islam as a potent force, the Islamists, on the other hand, underestimated the political role of the new social forces — and their demands — which had emerged in the wake of the long-term economic changes. The result, it now appears, was equally disastrous for both groups. The Islamists must therefore try to understand and analyze the sociopolitical reality of change along with developing prescriptive answers to the problems of their societies.

Finally, there is the issue of human rights. Islamic political theorists have generally treated this relatively abstract and have not tried to work out the modalities of their operational realization and procedural details. In this respect, modern Muslim political theorists have much to learn from the classical Muslim jurists. It should be remembered that these jurists elaborated a complex system of checks and safeguards in order to ensure the complete observance of both the substantive and procedural aspects of legality and justice as prescribed in the Qur'an and the traditions of the Prophet. These jurists, both inside and outside the state apparatuses, upheld the fundamental human rights of all citizens, irrespective of their creed, class or color, with legendary courage and conviction in the wake of often ruthless rulers. The classical jurists may be faulted for their less-than-ideal position with respect to the collective right of the community to rebel against a usurper, but when it came to the defense of an indiuvidual citizen's civil, economic, and cultural rights, they were uncompromisingly steadfast and firm. Not only did these jurists work out a theoretical framework within which the fundamental human rights of individuals became justifiable, they also used this framework as a basis for a legal order which supported by legislative measures, sought to ensure their implementation in concrete situations. As such, the question of human rights was not Universal Declaration of Human Rights and the International Covenant on Economic, Social, and Cultural Rights, which still remain moral recommendations not guaranteed by any legal safeguards, the classical Muslim jurists saw to it that the ideal code of human rights enunciated by Islam, which confers honor, dignity, and freedom on mankind and eliminates injustice, oppression, and exploitation, became guaranteed as a legal imperative, constituting an integral part of the shari'ah.

The theoretical position which underlies the jurists' passionate defense of human rights is firmly rooted in the belief that God, and God alone, is the Lawgiver and the source of all human rights. The belief that these rights are of divine origin instead of being a product of some social or political contract based on "general will" or societal consensus means that no ruler, government, parliament, or any other state authority can curtail or violate them in any way, nor can an individual surrender them to any worldly authority in exchange for material gains — as is the case in communist societies.

Given this central position accorded to human rights in the Islamic scheme of social and political relations, both the current lack of interest in this issue on the part of modern Muslim political theorists and the dismal record of most Muslim countries with regard to these rights becomes especially unfortunate. The gap between the ideals as prescribed in the Qur'an and the Sunnah and the reality in contemporary Muslim societies is probably nowhere as conspicuous as in the area of human rights. The rights to life, freedom, honor, equality before the law, justice, belief, thought and expression, free association, economic pursuits, protection of property, privacy, and movement are violated much more often than they are observed. We suggest that Muslim political scientists take up the issue of human rights as a priority item both in their research projects and on their political action agendas.

Indeed, [even before] did We send Our Messengers with all evidence of [this] truth; and sent down with them the Book and [thus gave you] a balance [with which to weigh right and wrong], so that men might behave with equity; and We gave [you the ability to make use of] iron, in which there is awesome power as well as [a source of] benefits for man: and [all this was given to you O Muhammad!] so that Allah might mark out those who would stand up for Him and His Messenger, even though He [Himself] is beyond the reach of human perception.

al-Hadīd: 25

[They are] those whom if We give authority in the land, they will establish worship and give regular charity, enjoin the right and forbid wrong: with Allah rests the end [and decision] of [all] affairs.

al-Hajj: 41

PROBLEMS OF ISLAMIC POLITICAL THEORY

Khalid M. Ishaque

The study of Islamic political theory is beset with serious problems for Muslim as well as non-Muslim scholars. For the Muslim student of this field, the situation is further complicated since he is compelled to study it under four distinct limitations.

Hadith, fiqh, early *rijal* (chain informants) material, and Qur'anic exegesis, all of which form the foundation of Islamic political literature, have acquired a hallow of sanctification. With the passage of time, the sanctification has intensified to the extent that a person today who rejects a hadith of Malik's *al-Muwatta'* runs the risk of being called a *munkir* (denier) of hadith, even though, according to az-Zarqani, Imam Malik used to revise his work and on verification would add or exclude material from it.

Some early personalities have acquired such a dominant position in Islamic studies that their decisions or views, even though their time frame has changed, are held to be sacrosanct, and anyone suggesting a change is charged with blasphemy.

For example, *talaq al-bid'ah* (the bad divorce) was an old *ad hoc* decision of Caliph 'Umar, arising out of a need to prevent people from abusing the right of divorce. It clearly appears to be contrary to the practice in effect during the days of the Prophet, upon whom be peace, but violent opposition was offered when the government of Pakistan sought to revive the Prophet's practice regarding talaq (divorce) in the Family Law Ordinance of 1961.

It must be recalled that during the last fourteen hundred years of Muslim history, sincere as well as ill-motivated innovations were made. Muslims were obviously wary of *ijtihad* because, by definition the generations closer in time to the Prophet were considered superior to those who succeeded them.

Besides, the period of decline, after a brilliant first one thousand years, was prolonged and agonizing. The 'ulema thought it best to preserve the *shari'ah* by claiming that ijtihad was no longer necessary. They felt morally secure in their secluded cloisters, away from the dirty politics of their governments. They sought to secure the shari'ah by insulating it, hoping that it would be brought out and applied by virtuous rulers in better days. One example of this isolationism and intellectual inactivity is that, even after seven centuries, the *al-Ahkam as-Sultaniyyah* of al-Mawardi and Abi Y'ala remain the best description of basic governmental and administrative Muslim institutions.

During the last three hundred years, the intellectual leadership of the civilized world has shifted to the West. The West undertook the study of Islam to familiarize itself with the ideology of a fallen enemy. It was therefore superficial and somewhat contemptuous. In the second stage, during the process of imperialistic consolidation, efforts were made to reveal Islam's inferiority in relation to other systems. This was followed by a new and sophisticated style which acknowledged past achievements but denied any contemporary relevance or intrinsic fairness to Islam. In recent times, the picture is singularly confused as so many people are pushing their own particular views. Even those who try to make a fair study of Islam are handicapped by their own prejudices and world views. Most of these scholars view the Qur'an as one of several books forming their source material. As such, they place a lot of emphasis on the earliest recorded interpretations of the Qur'an as the key to its correct appreciation.

Ironically, even those Muslim scholars who study Islam quite often borrow all the prejudices of their Western teachers. This practice of learning the Qur'an through old works is thereby reinforced, and historical precedents begin to acquire religious sanctity.

Al-Mawardi and Abu Y'ala, for example, speak of the valid forms of succession as: 'election' by the elite of the *ummah* (Abu Bakr's succession), nomination by an individual ('Umar's succession), nomination by a panel ('Uthman's election), and the *bai'ah* given by the people (Ali's succession). They also speak of a forcible acquisition of power, which by their times had become the standard technique. It is obvious that in the preceding formulations, theory follows the early practice and contemporary history. Here again, by implication, new forms are assumed to be excluded. So much praise is showered on the favored forms that the ummah is practically debarred from formulating any new methods of succession and no other historical or contemporary forms are recognized as worthy of emulation. In contrast, those who are impressed by Western institutions feel that the early Muslim forms are primitive, and that if they represent the zenith reached by the ummah, they are hardly worth all the praise they have received over the years.

We must, therefore, in fairness to Islam, state the basic issues of politics, and the means and methods by which political problems are resolved by it, as well as devise a correct approach toward understanding the Qur'an and Sunnah,

The basic tragedy of human existence, as Homer observed, lies in the strong taking what he wants and the weak surrendering what he must. There is justice only between equals, not between men. To Heraclitus, the greatest human tragedy lies in the fact that power does not recognize the superior claims of morality and that those who have knowledge or virtue have no share, or effective share, in power.

In other words, man's primary problems have been:
(a) how to subordinate power to morality,
(b) how to direct power into the hands of virtuous and knowledgeable people, and
(c) how to establish justice between men

Western political theory offers the following in response to this challenge: (1) democratic institutions, (2) separation of powers, (3) enforceable human rights, (4) independent superior judicial tribunals, (5) adult franchise, and (6) bureaucracy to enforce the will of the people.

Marxist-Leninism, on the basis of its analysis of social problems, offers the following solutions: (1) public ownership of the means of production, (2) dictatorship of the proletariat, (3) class struggle, and (4) guaranteed satisfaction of basic needs, with (5) bureaucracy as the means for achieving the desired results.

Notwithstanding the successes of the West in certain areas over limited periods, as well as the massive strides of the socialist world in some fields, both systems have run into various difficulties and have failed to meet the challenge of our times. Western liberalism believed that it could solve the problems of humanity through a network of sociopolitical institutions based on democratic principles. This was a very self-confident response made from the 19th century to the middle of the 20th century, but events of the last fifty years have shown that each of these institutions is subject to abuse and distortion and prospers only under certain socioeconomic and political conditions. For instance, Western style democracy only works effectively in communities (a) which have achieved a reasonably high standard of living for each group; (b) where there is a general consensus about overall national priorities between opposing political parties; (c) where people have a high standard of literacy; (d) where differences of race, color, language, and religion exist within a manageable range; and (e) where a state of mutual respect, trust in the national leadership, and a common aspiration for a shared future exist.

It is an historic fact that the British style of democracy found roots and became operational in Canada, Australia, and New Zealand, but failed to achieve similar success in many former British colonies in Asia and Africa. In some cases, it was due to poverty and cut-throat competition for limited resources; while in others, the future desired by contesting groups differed widely. Lack of consensus and a narrow political base often force immoral decisions on third-world leaders, and lack of political awareness only makes matters worse. Having no shared vision for the future and being disappointed with the rate of progress, people have sought security in smaller unions based on tribal, racial, religious, or linguistic subgroups.

Even in the developed democratic world, where the prerequisites for democracy exist, the institutions are not working as good as promised or hoped. The quality of public leadership has suffered a general decline; narrow group interests dominate the political process, and wealth and power successfully manipulate the democratic process.

The ideas of separation of power and the rule of law have also suffered erosion. With the aid of bureaucracy, the executive wing has become so powerful and sophisticated that national legislatures can no longer effectively control or guide it in even the most advanced democracies. The supremacy of executive power has enabled it to push through legislation to suit its own purposes. Enforceable human rights have been negated. The welfare state has almost obtained a monopoly of financial power. In the name of economic security, it has either taxed away (directly or through monetary measures) private property, or has placed it under so much regulation that it can no longer be characterized as private property. Individual privacy is also subject, in varying degrees, to legalized snooping, and freedom of thought and expression are threatened by propaganda and attempts to control people's minds.

Adult franchise is the other favorite theme which, unfortunately for contemporary politics, is the most abused. Even in countries with a respectable democratic past, manipulation of voters through direct or hidden persuasion, demagogy and bribery has created a situation in which votes — if not sold outright — are cast for the candidates most likely to prove useful for the individual voter's personal gains or for other collateral purposes. It is obvious that given a situation of crisis, the outcome would depend more on the intellectual and moral caliber of the participants than on the capability of institutions. Similar constitutions produce different results in different sociopolitical settings. Many countries with far more neatly drafted constitutions than America's do not even reach its standard of democracy.

If the Western capitalism-liberalism combination has not fully redeemed the promise of a great society, Marxism-Leninism has done no better. It started with the thesis that all social problems flow from private ownership of the means of production. To end these problems, all means of production had to be publicly owned by the bureaucrats exercising the *de facto* powers of the previous private owners. Under this new dispensation, the life style of the people was no better than under the previous one. In fact, in some sense, it was worse under the dictatorship of the proletariat. However, after sixty-three years of proletarian dictatorship, the class struggle still goes on even in the USSR. No socialist state has succeeded in reaching the standard of living achieved by even a second-rate capitalist country. Regulation and regimentation have reached strangulating dimensions and the promised 'withering away of the state' is nowhere in sight. The price that people have paid in loss of liberty, dignity, and spirituality is so great that the socialist government must use every conceivable type of coercion to keep its citizens from trying to leave the 'socialist paradise.' Lastly, if bureaucracy is oppressive all-pervading in the capitalist welfare state, it is even more powerful and insufferable in the socialist world. Corruption and crime are rampant under both systems. From an Islamic point of view, some further criticism would also be in order.

Both the liberal-democratic and the socialist systems are essentially secular and materialistic and, as a consequence, lack the spiritual anchorage necessary for developing the two ingredients crucial for raising human life above an animal existence – that is, first, the will to resist and fight evil, and second, a genuine compassion and honor for fellow beings. The only foundation for the first is faith in one God, in the life hereafter, and the ultimate reckoning; and for the second, a world view which, for spiritual advancement, makes human society a field for moral endeavor.

Secular philosophies are considered successful to the degree that they keep their populations happy and materially well-off. People prefer immediate satisfactions to long-term programs of a shared future with others because life is short and fleeting. Seen from this point of view, another individual, if he is not a source of satisfaction, becomes a nuisance because he also seeks to obtain society's limited resources. Without genuine compassion and regard for human dignity, charity through bureaucracy is nothing but a distribution of crumbs by a faceless machine. It does not bind but divides, hurting the recipients in their very souls.

On the other hand, everyone living under secular systems is justified in asking for immediate gratification as opposed to the prophets in the Qur'an who say:

> I seek no recompense from you, my recompense is with none but Allah.

It is the prophetic approach alone which gives an abiding strength to the idea of putting one's obligations before one's rights, and the will to sacrifice immediate gains for a better tomorrow.

The inner logic of a secular approach to life compels people to insist on their rights first, but it is common knowledge that the edifice of human civilization is built on the efforts of those who have willingly given more to mankind than they have taken of it. By the same token, communities which have collectively remained aware of the priorities of their duties and obligations over their rights have done better than those who have insisted on their rights first. The body develops through acquisitiveness, the soul through willing sacrifice.

If that is the case, what is Islam's response to these problems which it treats as a part of its total response to the existential challenge that faces mankind?

According to Islam, whatever is in heaven and earth belongs to Allah the Creator, the Sustainer, the Guide, the Reckoner, and the Lawgiver. He has endowed human beings with different capabilities and a field of endeavor. He will, both in this world and in the hereafter, call every person to account for how he used his capabilities. Accountability is the very lifeblood of Islam's vision of the life in this world.

To succeed on the day of reckoning and to find fulfillment, salvation, and abundance, every person must renew his primordial covenant with Allah[1] in this world[2] and agree to use his life and all his possessions in the service of, and in accordance with, the priorities fixed by Allah.[3] Therefore, his obligations must precede his rights, and he must concentrate on fulfilling them irrespective of others' attitudes.[4] To follow divine guidance – that is, to aspire for the objectives which Allah prescribes, by the methods that He

---

[1] The Qur'an 7:172
[2] The Qur'an 48:10
[3] The Qur'an 9:111
[4] The Qur'an 5:105

ordains or recommends and within the limits set out by Him —
is to live in a new dimension of existence. Every man must view
his capabilities as a trust and with the clear perception that the
greater one's capabilities, the greater one's accountability. The
political implication of the preceding principles is in relation to
the ultimate sovereignty of Allah, which determines the objectives
as well as the limitations of political power. Human efforts and
exercise of political authority are subordinate to the shari'ah. The
shari'ah is the guide as well as the criterion for judging human
actions at their legislative, administrative, and judicial levels.
Power is subordinate to law, and both law and morality emanate
from the same source. Law must protect the pre-eminence of morality.

A corollary of the preceding commitment is the second constitutional principle that there is no obedience to or cooperation with,
or rendering assistance to any human agency if it involves dis-
obeying the divine mandate.[5] Every Muslim is bound to obey the
divine command; to obey or cooperate with others is only part of
his obligation to Allah. It took many holocausts and wars to make
the West realize the wisdom of the Prophet's statement that "there
is no obedience of a human being in that which entails disobedience to Allah," and the Qur'anic verse:

> Aid each other in [what is] good and moral, and do not
> aid each other in [what is] sinful or [involves] transgres-
> sion.[6]

According to the Qur'an, power is a gift to the ummah for its
good deeds.[7] By the same token, it is withdrawn when the
ummah falls below the minimum standards laid down by Him.
The Qur'an stipulates:

> Allah has promised those among you who believe and
> do good work that He will surely give them authority in
> this earth as He gave to those before them and that He
> will surely establish for them the *deen* [way of life] which
> He has chosen for them; and that He will surely give them
> in exchange of fear, security [peace].[8]

When vested in individuals, power, like wealth or knowledge,
is a trust and is to be exercised in accordance with the priorities
and limits set by Allah. It is significant that one's obedience is

---

[5]The Qur'an 68:10-15; 76:24; 26:151-152
[6]The Qur'an 5:2
[7]The Qur'an 5:8
[8]The Qur'an 24:55

conditional and that the right to protest is guaranteed, as are the principles by which it is to be resolved. In a Qur'anic verse,[9] people in authority are ordered to discharge their trusts and to be fair while deciding disputes. In the following verse, people are ordered to obey Allah and to obey His Prophet and also those among them who are in authority. Should a dispute arise with others or with the rulers, the criteria provided by Allah and His Prophet decide the matter.

Another equally important aspect of this right is that no ruler is entitled to any privilege which would make him immune to the law and the people. This is why Abu Bakr, the first caliph, said when he assumed this post:

> O people, I have been made the ruler among you, and
> I am not the best of you. So if I act rightly, help me, and
> if I am in error, correct me.

'Authority on earth' is given to the ummah, and the rulers of the day exercise it as its agents.

The rulers are therefore accountable to the people, and by the same token, they become liable to correction and removal by them. In Islamic law, there is no validation of illegal acts legislated by parliaments or rulers.

There is a hadith reported from the Prophet, upon whom be peace, that one should help his brother when he acts rightly and also when he acts wrongly. His companions understood helping one in goodness but they were confused about helping one in error. The Prophet is reported to have said: "You can do so by setting him right." This hadith makes it the people's duty to correct the authorities.

Participation in the ummah's affairs, to prevent abuse of power, is both an obligation and a right of every Muslim. By definition, the ummah is a community of believers who are true to their covenant with Allah and persevere in the performance of their obligations.

It was under this inspiration that fairly early in Muslim history, *Qadi* courts, *Nazr al-Mazalim* (small cause) tribunals, institutions of *al-Hisbah* (ombudsman), and *Wizara* came into effective existence. The ummah is under obligation to devise and build institutions to enforce these principles of the shari'ah so that the creative impulses of the people are given free expression. The protection

---

[9] The Qur'an 4:58

of human rights has a special place in the structure of Islamic society. The Prophet, while calling Allah and the entire ummah as witnesses, spoke of the fulfillment of his mandate in terms of the inviolability of human rights to life, honor, and possessions. After quoting the Qur'anic verse: "O mankind! We have created you from a male and a female, and We have made you into families and tribes that you may recognize one another. Verily, the most honorable in the sight of Allah is he who is most righteous among you," he said:

A colored man has no preference over a white man, nor a white man over a colored one, nor an Arab over a non-Arab, nor a non-Arab over an Arab, except for righteousness.

O people, your lives, your honor, and your properties are to be respected by one another until the Day of Reckoning comes. They are to be respected as you respect this day (Yum 'Arfah) and this month (Dhul-Hajjah) in this city.

By the same token, these rights cannot be taken away from individual Muslims by the collective will of the ummah or by any individual exercising political power.

In its long history, the ummah may not have always lived up to these high ideals, but these latter have always been there, forever beckoning each new generation of Muslims to realize them. The challenge for the ummah, therefore, is to either adapt the old institutions or to devise new ones to assure (1) that the shari'ah becomes the supreme law of the land; (2) that everyone is treated in accordance with laws that project and enforce the shari'ah; (3) that the rights belonging to individuals are protected and that adequate institutions exist for such protection; (4) that people are not compelled to obey secular laws which involve disobedience to the shari'ah; (5) that the right to protest and seek adjudication through an independent tribunal is assured to everyone; (6) that all public and private authorities act with justice and equality; and (7) that shura, as a principle of decision making and governance of public affairs, is made truly operational.

Like justice, equality is also a key concept in Islam. The constituents of this equality require that each person be treated as equal with regards to his opportunity, protection, dignity, security of life, honor, and property. However, this equality is not one of equal outcome for all. Islam's other principles of fair wages for what one does include such a consequence. It is not Islam's intention to steamroll everyone into a state of unmerited absolute equality since for each individual, there is a recompense equal to his efforts.[10] It, however, tempers the harshness of merited returns with the principle of compassion and mercy. Compassion must always accompany justice.[11] The strong must protect the weak, and the honored must lift the fallen.

The Qur'an makes clear provisions for those entitled to honor and authority within the ummah. These prerequisites encompass superior moral conduct,[12] which means a display of moral rectitude in the face of dangers or temptations, and the rendering of greater services to the community of believers; greater knowledge;[13] and physical competence.[14] On the other hand, the ummah should see to it that only those who are knowledgeable and physically fit to discharge their obligations should be allowed to run its affairs. The Qur'an clearly says that those who accepted Islam before its final victory were superior to those who accepted it afterwards.[15] In other words, the Qur'an prescribes the route to status within the ummah, and every member of it must willingly accept the superiority of those who are entitled to it. Conflict or confusion in this area causes the ultimate collapse of every institution — even in the most united and compact of communities. It is, therefore, not surprising that when the elite of Muhajireen (emigrants) and Ansar (the helpers) elected Abu Bakr, the whole community followed suit. The contemporary confusion and dispute about elections, representations, and voting arise because of the absence of criteria for leadership and decision making in the community. As for leading people and devising institutions to advance those values fixed by Allah, the role of leadership is clear cut and straightforward. Once it is assured that morally and intellectually superior individuals are available for service, a large number of voting and other political practices which have been abused in the past could be avoided.

Once elected, the ruling elites in a secular democracy are not answerable to anyone (except the voter in the next election several years away). So long as they act within a facade of legality, they can legitimately use their office for advancing their personal careers. Laws favoring some and discriminating against others

---

[10]The Qur'an 16:90
[11]The Qur'an 49:13
[12]The Qur'an 39:9
[13]The Qur'an 2:247
[14]Ibid
[15]The Qur'an 57:10

are passed. Lobbies of hidden persuaders continue to cause distortions in priorities. A realistic assessment of contemporary elected legislators' conduct leads one to agree with Marx that the law is a tool of the ruling elite – that is, those who are economically powerful.

Under the Islamic system, the objectives which law aspires to achieve and the values it endeavors to sustain and advance are already given. The scope of legislative activity is, therefore, limited to discovering the means to achieve them. It is further hedged in by the protections given to every individual to protest and seek independent adjudication if he thinks his rights, as assured by the shari'ah, have been violated. No legislature under the Islamic system can suspend or abrogate this right. In fact, a system would cease to be Islamic if there is an infringment of this right. What needs to be done is to devise powerful institutions to protect these divinely given rights and to assure election of persons with superior qualities to public office so they can advance the values which the Qur'an and the Sunnah demand.

The Qur'an has described in various places the qualities of those who must be accorded honor and be entrusted with authority. These are the people who have distinguished themselves in the service of Islam in times of adversity; people who are intellectually, morally, and physically able to discharge their duties; and people who have proved their trustworthiness in the past. These qualities can become the criteria for electing a truly Islamic shura. In an Islamic state, these stringent qualifications would be required of upon an aspiring legislator. Surely, in a truly Muslim community, mere inherited wealth, family relations, or flexibility to promise everything to everyone does not and cannot qualify any person for membership in the shura.

Since temporal authority is a gift from God to the ummah for its good deeds, Muslims have been told to settle their affairs through shura or mutual consultation (ash-Shura: 38). Mutual consultation means a mutually trustful dialogue between two or more individuals ending in an agreement to pursue a common course of action. In fact, the root meaning of the word shura is related to the process of drawing honey from a honeycomb. In other words, public authority is a trust given to the person or persons in behalf of the ummah to decide upon a course of conduct by mutual consultation. Even the Prophet, upon whom be peace, was asked to constantly pray for an increase in knowledge (Taha: 14) and to consult the ummah on the issues (āl-'Imrān: 159). The Qur'an does not give the right to anyone, including the prophets, to become authoritarian and deprive people of their right to think for themselves. The Qur'an states it very clearly that it would not be right for a person that Allah give him dominion and prophethood, and then he should say to mankind: "Be slaves unto me and not to Allah," but he should say: "Be solely devoted to Allah, because you know the Book and because you study [it]" (āl-'Imrān: 79).

Any person who claims the authority to reject the advice given by shura goes against the mandates of the Qur'an and the Sunnah. If the prophets have not been given the authority to enslave people, how can a government — no matter how highly rated — claim this status? The Prophet is reported to have said to Abu Bakr and 'Umar that if they agreed on a course of action, then he could not oppose them.

In summary, the Qur'an seems to require that authority be vested in people who can rule through ability and competency, not through gimmickery. It treats power as a trust and draws up the basic rules to exercise it. It makes every person, no matter how high or low, accountable for all his capabilities; it requires power to be used to aid justice and mercy. The life of this world is the route through which everyone must pass, in a manner in which he does so will win him his hereafter.

Having traversed this wide field, one can now clearly see that salvation, success, prosperity, and happiness in Islam means something much more extensive, higher, and nobler than the secular definition of the good life in liberal democratic and socialist systems. This difference has to be understood because any program for social change and development within a community succeeds to the extent that it avoids a dichotomy between the word and the deed. Some of the Muslim world's major problems arise from the fact that those who de facto exercise power do not always agree with the priorities of the shari'ah. The ummah's task is to change the rhetoric of Islamic idealism into practical programs which can effect all the legislative, judicial, and executive processes of the state, particularly in regard to their priorities.

THE CONCEPT OF STATE IN ISLAM

Justice Javid Iqbal

The state in Islam is founded on certain principles as laid down in the Qur'an and Sunnah of the Prophet Muhammad, upon whom be peace. The first principle is that all authority in the universe lies with Allah because He alone created it. Thus, according to a Muslim's faith, only Allah is to be obeyed; man can be obeyed only if Allah commands it. The second principle is that Islamic law has already been legislated in the Qur'an by Allah and in the Sunnah of the Prophet, the latter being the authoritative exposition of the Qur'an. These injunctions have, for the guidance of mankind, been sent form time to time to the Prophets, the last being the Prophet Muhammad, upon whom be peace, through whom the faith was perfected. Allah has already placed the knowledge of good and evil in the nature of man and has further clarified it in the Qur'an by means of *awamar* and *nawahi* (the positive and negative injunctions of the Qur'an). Based on these beliefs, Muslims have always understood that they are to enforce the already existing regulations in all spheres of their life, rather than creating "new" laws.

The Qur'an ordains no specific mode of life for a politically and economically subjugated Muslim community. In an-Nisa': 59, Muslims are commanded to obey Allah, the Prophet, and those among them who are in authority, provided they are adhering to the commandments of Allah and the Prophet. Obviously, rendering obedience to those who command authority over the Muslim community is conditional and ceases if the preceding condition is not fulfilled. It is further evident that this mode of life can only be followed if Muslims live in a politically and economically free community. As such, the Muslim community must strive for establishing a state wherever possible.

A state which is administered in accordance with Islamic law is technically called *darul Islam* (country of peace). If an Islamic state is politically or economically subjugated by a non-Muslim power, it will be transformed into *darul harb* (country of war), and the Muslims would be left with only two alternatives: either to conduct *jihad* (struggle) in order to regain their independent status, or to migrate (*hijrah*) to some Muslim country. Thus, the Muslims' concept of patriotism is not based solely on their attachment to a particular territory, but rather on the ideals and aspirations embodied in the institutions they establish in that Muslim territory.

In theory, the Islamic state is Allah's state, and the Muslims are His party (*hizbullah*). This is based on a twofold concept of happiness (*falah*): (1) it must work for the success of the Muslim community in this world as well as prepare it for success in the hereafter; and (2) to realize these objectives, the Muslim community (*ummah*) must be based on the principles of equality, solidarity, and freedom.

Traditionally, Muslim jurists have emphasized three important features of an Islamic state: the Muslim community (*ummah*), the Islamic law (*shari'ah*), and the leadership of the Muslim community (*khalifah*). Since absolute authority or ultimate sovereignty rests in Allah, the Islamic state must uphold the supremacy of Islamic law; furthermore, since the Muslim community is to be governed in accordance with the Islamic law, it must have a directing head to implement or execute it. This head of state has no inherent power to legislate, for his sole responsibility is to implement the Qur'anic law. However, guided by the spirit of those laws and principles, he is authorized, in certain exceptional circumstances, to alter or temporarily suspend those laws or make subordinate legislation. To do so, he first of all has to appoint a body of advisers (*shura*) and then consult its individual members to determine the proper subordinate legislation. However, he is not bound by their advice.

The head of the Muslim community is called *khalifah* (the successor of the Prophet) or imam. The judiciary (*qada'*) has the power to interpret the Islamic law and to adjudicate cases according to its precepts. In the majority view, as shall be explained later, the appointment of the khalifah or caliph confirmed by the Muslim community through *bai'ah* (a symbolic way of rendering obedience), which is a contract between the two concerned parties — the ruler and the ruled. The Muslim community is to render obedience to the caliph who in turn promises to govern the Muslim community in conformity with the Islamic law. Disputes between the parties, according to injunction,[1] are to be referred to the judiciary for adjudication. Its decision, based on the Book of Allah and the Sunnah of the Prophet, is binding on both parties. If the dispute cannot be resolved through peaceful means, the Muslim community or any of its members is entitled to rebel against the erring khalifah or to replace him by another (imam).

Theoretically speaking, the ruler of an Islamic state does not enjoy absolute authority, neither do the parliament or the people, for this can belong only to Allah, and His law must remain supreme. Using today's terminology, the Islamic constitution has only two important organs: the executive and the judiciary. The possible third organ – that is, the legislative is constitutionally undefined because all legislation has already been laid down by Allah in the Qur'an. It is the government's duty to implement it, not to alter it in its own interest. Should there be a need for legislation on issues not specified by the shari'ah, it can be enacted after due process of consultation with the shura.

There are two verses in the Qur'an about consultation. In ash-Shura: 38, it is said that the Muslims conduct their affairs by mutual consultations, and in āl-'Imrān: 159, the Prophet is commanded to consult with the people in the community to carry out the resulting decision after placing his trust in Allah. In the first verse, consultation is only recommended, meaning that it is not obligatory. However, it is characteristic of the Muslim community to run its affairs by mutual consultation. The second verse, addressed to the Prophet, contains the instruction that those who command authority should consult the community on all matters of importance.

The main distinction between an Islamic state and a secular state is that the former is governed by the laws of Allah as revealed in the Qur'an, whereas the latter is governed by man-made laws. The other distinction is that a modern secular state should have three features: it must be fully sovereign, be national, and have a well-defined territory. When these three features exist, a state can legitimately proclaim itself as a sovereign state. However, an Islamic state, although sovereign according to these criteria, is theoretically not fully sovereign because this attribute can only be applied to Allah. Strictly speaking, it is also not a national state, for a Muslim community is based on faith and consists of people who may belong to different tribes, races, or nationalities; speak different languages; or be of a different color. What all of them have in common is their spiritual aspiration – that is, their faith in Islam — and that they regard themselves as a nation because of this common spiritual aspiration. However, if nationalism is to be considered in Western terms, then an Islamic state is a multinational state. Third, it is not a territorial state in the strict sense of the term because it aspires to become a universal state. Nevertheless, it is not a utopia or an imaginary state; it has to be initially founded as a territorial state.

The Prophet migrated from his ancestral home, Makkah, and established the Islamic state at Medinah by uniting the immigrants and helpers in fraternal bond of brotherhood based on faith. Afterwards, the territories of the Islamic state continued to expand.

In an-Nisa': 58, Muslims are commanded by Allah to hand over their trust only to the most competent persons. In other words, the Qur'an has ordained that only the most competent person/persons be appointed to rule the Islamic state. Yet, the Qur'an itself does not lay down any specific method for appointing a caliph. This was quite natural because the Qur'an is concerned mainly with matters relating to right and wrong or good and evil, not with matters relating to planning (*tadbir*). The appointment of the best person/persons is a matter relating to right and wrong, even at that, the question as to how the appointment is to be made, or whether a particular selection process is correct or not, is a matter to be solved by human intelligence in light of the prevailing conditions. Similarly, no procedure has been prescribed for removing a caliph. According to the majority view, the Prophet did not nominate or appoint any successor after him, nor did he lay down any rule or method for constituting or deposing his successor. These structures were to evolve according to the wisdom and needs of the community and were not meant to be permanent, for different times and conditions require different solutions. Consequently, the real objective of Islam is to establish a community of faith governed by the shari'ah. How it enforces the shari'ah is a matter for communal decision.

Some modern Muslim thinkers cynically state that since Allah mentions kings in the Qur'an, monarchy is an approved institution. The argument proceeds further: the Prophet of Islam was a prophet-king in the tradition of the earlier prophet-kings mentioned in the Qur'an. This argument finds support in the writings of Al-Farabi who, influenced by Plato's theory of the philosopher-king, developed his concept of the prophet-imam (king). He applied it to the Prophet of Islam and described his period of imamate in Medinah as the ideal state. In other words, according to al-Farabi, the ideal Islamic state was established at Medinah by the Prophet of Islam and, as long as he remained its prophet-imam, the twofold concept of happiness would be fully realized by the Muslim community. Apart from the idealistic or philosophical implications of this thesis, it may be categorically stated that in the Qur'an, Allah talks of kings who might have lived before the advent of Islam and that, although the institution of monarchy has not been specifically condemned, it is clearly stated in ash-Shura: 38 that Muslims are to conduct their affairs by mutual consultation. One could say that this verse does not make consultation an obligation, but it must also not be forgotten that the verse is describing the nature of the Muslim community which, according to Allah, conducts its affairs by mutual consultation. The second objection to this argument is that the Prophet of Islam never claimed to be a prophet-king. He has not been appointed as such by Allah as was the Prophet David, who was specifically appointed Allah's successor on earth. Nevertheless, there are numerous commands in the Qur'an addressed to the Prophet which order him to consult with the community. One example is found in āl-Imrān: 159: "Consult them in affairs, and when you have made a decision, put your trust in Allah." The Islamic state in Medinah was based on the contract of Medinah, by which the contracting parties agreed to run the government with the Prophet as the sole arbiter and as the apex of delegated sovereignty.

The principles which can be deduced from this arrangement are: the sovereignty of Allah and Supremacy of His law, the union of the immigrants and helpers on the fraternal bond of faith, the establishment of the Islamic state at Medinah as well as its administration in accordance with Islamic law. The Prophet was the head or imam of the Muslim community, but his only kingly prerogatives was that his seal conferred legitimacy to state documents. Furthermore, since he had been commanded to consult the eminent members of the Muslim community (his companions) in managing the community's affairs, he did so. These companions of the Prophet have been described as those who had the authority to loosen and bind (ahlal-hall wal 'aqd) and had apparently formed an informal senate.

However, as stated earlier, the majority view holds that the Prophet neither nominated or appointed any successor, nor laid down any procedure or framework for installing or replacing his successor. Jalaluddin Suyuti (on the authority of Hudayfah) states that some of the Prophet's companions asked him to appoint a successor. He refused to do so, saying that if they were to rebel against the successor appointed by him, they would be punished. Had he in fact appointed a successor or detailed a specific mode of selection, then that mode alone would have become the only way of appointing the head of state, and a restrictive stipulation of this nature would have caused great difficulty in the evolution of Islamic polity. Thus, by not appointing his successor or suggesting any specific mode, the Prophet acted in conformity with the spirit of Qur'anic injunctions pertaining to this matter.

During the period of the first four rightly guided caliphs (632 C.E. to 661 C.E.), different methods were adopted for the appointment of the caliph. In all cases, the appointment was confirmed by the bai'ah of the Muslim community. In general, the methods adopted during this period had a common feature – that is, the selection of the best man through initial election, nomination, and election through an electoral college, followed by private bai'ah and confirmation through a public bai'ah. The course adopted in these cases was republican, although the majority principle, not specifically disapproved, had not been followed.

After the death of the Prophet, Muslims in Medinah formed distinct political groups such as Ansar, Muhajirin, and Banu Hashim. The groups had their respective leaders. The Ansar were led by S'ad ibn 'Ubadah, the Muhajirin supported Abu Bakr and 'Umar, whereas the Banu Hashim were solidly behind 'Ali. Ibn Ishaq's biography of the Prophet, written within seventy years of his death, gives an accurate picture of the election of the first caliph, Abu Bakr. The Ansar claimed power on the grounds that they constituted the bulk of the Muslim armed forces. They even suggested as an alternative the divisibility of delegated sovereignty. The Muhajirin stood for Muslim communal unity and claimed power on the grounds that all Arabs would only accept leadership from the tribe of Quraysh. The claim of the Banu Hashim was based on their connection with the family of the Prophet. The groups, with the exception of the Banu Hashim, gathered in the hall of Banu Sa'adah and convened a political debate. Eventually, 'Umar proposed Abu Bakr and asked the latter to extend his hand, which he did, thereby accepting the nomination. After this, the Muhajirin and the Ansar present swore allegiance (bai'ah) to him. This private bai'ah was followed by a public bai'ah. It should be pointed out that in support of their respective claims, neither the Ansar nor the Muhajirin employed any Qur'anic injunction or any direction of the Prophet. The discussion was conducted as a conference which sought to maintain a dialogue for political consensus, realized through mutual consultation.

The second caliph, 'Umar, was nominated by Abu Bakr. The nomination had no legal precedence — it was merely a recommendation. Nevertheless, since the Muslim community had placed its confidence in Abu Bakr, his recommendation was accepted by the people of Medinah through a referendum, followed by a general bai'ah.

Reacting to the sociopolitical conditions of his time, 'Umar, before his death, formed an electoral college of the probable candidates and told them to elect one of them as his successor. This electoral college consisted of 'Ali, 'Uthman, 'Abdur Rahman, Sa'd, Zubair and Talhah. He also appointed his son 'Abdullah to cast the deciding vote in case there was a tie. He nevertheless excluded 'Abdullah from being his successor. The council, through a process of elimination, authorized 'Abdur Rahman to recommend whether 'Ali or 'Uthman should succeed 'Umar. 'Abdur Rahman is reported to have consulted as many people as he could in Medinah, including women, students, and those who came from outside or who happened to be present in Medinah as wayfarers. The majority of them supported 'Uthman. 'Abdur Rahman even interviewed 'Ali and 'Uthman about how they would rule the state if one of them became the leader. Eventually, 'Abdur Rahman supported 'Uthman and he was finally selected as the sole candidate. Later, the rest of the Muslim community swore allegiance to him.

After the assassination of 'Uthman, the people of Medinah gathered in 'Ali's house and requested him to become the successor. The Prophet's uncle, 'Abbas, supported him as the sole candidate. 'Ali refused to accept a private bai'ah and insisted that if the Muslim community wanted to swear allegiance to him as the khalifah, it should be openly done in the Prophet's mosque. This was done accordingly.

It is, therefore, evident that the first four leaders of the Muslim community could only be appointed with the consent of the people whom he would rule. Women were not excluded from this process and, according to some jurists, a woman can even stand as a candidate for the succession. Furthermore, it should be pointed out that hereditary succession was specifically excluded. In the early days of the Islamic state, the khalifah enjoyed only one privilege – that is, all the state documents had to bear his seal to be considered valid. In the turbulent days of 'Ali, a second prerogative was introduced: if the khalifah was not leading the congregational prayers, then the imam mentioned his name in the *khutbah* and prayed for him.

In the process of transformation from 661 C.E. to 1258 C.E., the interaction of numerous forces and events led to fundamental changes in the caliphate. Mu'awiyah was proclaimed khalifah in 661 C.E. Jurists like Shah Wali Ullah regard his method of selection as an appointment through usurpation (*istilā*)¹ because, according to him, it was obtained through coercion. Nevertheless, Shah Wali Ullah considers it as one of the legitimate or legally acknowledged methods of appointment. Four years before his death, Mu'awiyah successfully nominated his son Yazid to succeed him. The oath of allegiance was secured for him in spite of juristic protests maintaining that it was illegal to swear allegiance to two persons at the same time. Mu'awiyyah explained his action by claiming that if he had nominated anyone outside his own family, or if he had appointed a council as 'Umar had done, or

if he had left the matter to be decided by the community, it would
have led to civil war.

Addressing the peoples' concern, Marwan (his governor of
Medinah) said: "Verily, the commander of the faithful has seen fit
to appoint his son Yazid as the successor over you according to
the institutions of Abu Bakr and 'Umar." 'Abdur Rahman ibn Abu
Bakr interrupted: "Rather according to the institutions of Khusrau
and Caesar, for Abu Bakr and 'Umar did not nominate their chil-
dren, nor any member of their house." A prompt reply came from
Marwan: "There was no legal bar for Abu Bakr and 'Umar to do
so had they been found competent. But in the present case, the
commander of the faithful is nominating his son Yazid as successor over you because he has found him fit and competent."

This example, once set, was followed throughout the later history of Islam. The reigning caliph usually nominated one of his
sons or kinsmen as his successor, and the oath of allegiance was
secured for him. During the 'Abbassid rule, double nominations
were made – that is, two successors to hold the office, one after
the other, an arrangement which frequently led to wars of succession. Kingly prerogatives were also gradually introduced. Besides the earlier two prerogatives, namely, khatam (seal) and
khutbah(Friday speach), four more were introduced by
Mu'awiyah: the sarir (throne), the right of the caliph to sit at a
higher place (maqsura), the right to have an enclosure in the
mosque for his exclusive use, and finally, sikkah (currency) the
right to have his name carved on the country's coins. Arabic was
made the court language, and the earlier simplicity gradually
gave way to luxury and splendor.

The only reason advanced for the transformation of a republican or democratic form of government into a hereditary or dynastic monarchy was to avoid communal disintegration through per-
petual civil strife. Accepting the validity of this argument, Muslim
jurists began to provide rationales to bridge the gulf between the
ideal and the reality of their situation in order to maintain the
continuity of the community's character. Therefore, if the period
of the rightly guided caliphs illustrated the ideal Islamic polity,
the development of later constitutional thought represented the rational justification of the formal and substantial departure from
the ideal under the pressure of circumstances. It is interesting to
note that from this period onward, according to the majority of
the jurists, the replacement of a caliph by someone else through
coercion or usurpation (istila') was considered legitimate. Here it
should be mentioned that some jurists, Shah Wali Ullah for example, believe that a caliph or imam can only be selected according

to those methods used during the times of the rightly guided caliphs or through usurpation (istila'). The contemporary Muslim position is that the adaptation of different methods should not be considered as having any restrictive significance but rather as indicating a liberal and flexible approach – that is, the acceptability of adopting a method which is most suitable for realizing the objectives of the community at a particular time. According to al-Mawardi, the rule of a usurping emir is legitimate if he governs in accordance with the Islamic law. Such an idea can probably be traced to the doctrine of necessity as propounded by al-Ghazzali, who maintained that the tyranny of a usurping emir was preferable to chaos. Some jurists are of the opinion that since the usurping emir's source of strength is his own power, he does not require the consent of the Muslim community, while others think that the approval of the Muslim community is still required.

As long as the Muslim world remained united, it was administered by a universal caliphate, even though that institution had been transformed into a hereditary or dynastic monarchy. There are instances in the history of Islam when more than one caliphate was in existence at the same time, for example, those in Baghdad, Cairo, and Cordova. Still, even during that period, only the one in Baghdad eventually survived. At the time when Baghdad was sacked by the Mongols and the 'Abbassid caliph was put to death (1258 C.E.), there was no caliph anywhere in the Islamic world for a period of three years (1258 61 C.E.). In the later period of Islamic history, when numerous rulers managed to acquire power or controlled specific Muslim territories and the universal caliphate existed in name only, these rulers did not adopt the title of caliph or imam, but remained content to call themselves emirs, sultans, and padshahs.

The modern revival of Islam began in the 18th century with the gradual emergence of numerous independent or semi-independent national states in the Muslim world. In some of them, hereditary or dynastic monarchy was the order of the day, while in the others, legislative assemblies were constituted. Thus, when Muslims entered modern history, the question arose whether, in the absence of a universal caliphate, different Muslim national communities could manage their own affairs. In other words, could the powers and obligations of a khalifah or imam be shared by an elected body of people in a particular Muslim national state?

After the breakup of the Ottoman empire and the abolition of the caliphate in Constantinople (1924), Turkey was the first country in the world of Islam which actually transferred power of the caliph or imam to an elected assembly. This had also been the viewpoint of the khawaraj who, centuries earlier, had held that Muslims could manage their affairs by mutual consultation as recommended by the Qur'an. Others maintained that elected assemblies in modern Muslim national states could rule by way of *ijma'* or shura, make subordinate legislation on the basis of *ijtihad*, and interpret Islamic law in light of the changing needs and requirements of the Muslim community. In any case, no voice was raised against Turkey's action and legislative assemblies in other Muslim countries have never been considered repugnant to the injunctions of Islam.

Be that as it may, a Muslim national state does not become an Islamic state unless it adopts the Islamic method of governance, which remains unalterable. The democratic method adopted by some Muslim countries due to Western influence is admittedly not a perfect method. An Islamic state is expected to be run by the best members of the community, and the democratic method, although adopted by Western countries in order to achieve the same objective, ordinarily does not ensure the election of such people because it is the number of votes each candidate receives that determines who will rule. Similarly, a vote is no substitute for the bai'ah because it does not involve mutual obligations as does the latter. Furthermore, according to the sunnah of the Prophet, a person who presents himself as a candidate for any office abuses his position of trust (*kha'in*) and must be ignored. If this rule is adopted for the selection of a judge, then why should it not be adopted for the election of a legislator? Again, there is no obligation to follow the majority, as the majority right is not recognized in Islam. The supporters of this viewpoint also argue that since Muslims constitute Allah's party, the multi-party system can have no place in an Islamic state. It is also said that some Sunni schools of law do not acknowledge ijma' as a source for the evolution of Islamic law, but take shura as being merely a body of advisers or experts which must be appointed by the caliph through selection or nomination, and not election for the purpose of consultation.

The arguments advanced in favor of the democratic method are – that if the powers and obligations of a caliph or imam are to be shared by the community, there must be a group of people to carry out ijma' or shura in order to conduct the affairs of the Muslim community through mutual consultation. Such a body can only be established through the elected representatives of the Muslim community. Although the majority principle was not followed during the historical experiment of the rightly guided caliphs, its adaptation has neither been specifically forbidden nor disapproved of in the Qur'an and Sunnah. Admittedly, the Qur'an and Sunnah insist on the sovereignty of Allah and the enforcement of His laws, but the method for realizing these objectives is left to the good sense of the Muslim community. As the real objective of Islam is to establish a community of faith governed by the shari'ah, Muslims are free to develop any suitable method for its enforcement. The principle of ignoring a candidate who nominates himself is not practical, for if all suitable and competent persons kept quiet, then the Muslim community, being unaware of their presence, would be compelled to select mediocreones to guide its affairs. Furthermore, even though a vote is not a bilateral covenant like the bai'ah, it is certainly an indication in favor of one candidate over the others and is based on his competency. If he proves to be unsuitable or incompetent, he can be replaced at the next election. The establishment of a legislature is also necessary because subordinate legislation is a very wide field, for the changing needs and requirements of present-day life must be met. The successful working of the democratic method really depends on a conscientious electorate, aware of its rights and obligations under the Islamic law. It is likely to fail where the electorate is gullible. Therefore, it is necessary to educate and train the Muslim community so that it will not be deceived and elect unqualified people. It is also argued that although the Muslim community is Allah's party, the formation of groups to promote good and suppress evil is recommended by the Qur'an and Sunnah. Such a development has a historical precedent: soon after the death of the Holy Prophet, three distinct political groups emerged from the Muslim community, namely, the Ansar, the Muhajirin, and the Banu Hashim. During the caliphate of 'Ali, two more political groups were formed, namely, shi'an-i 'Ali and khawaraj. No objections were raised about any of these groups. Therefore, political parties are permitted to function in a Muslim national state provided they adhere to the Islamic ideology and operate strictly within its framework. However, to ascertain the will of the Muslim community, measures can be adopted to determine which candidate obtains an overwhelming (and not merely bare) majority of votes. It is further argued that the democratic method must be adopted, because there is, at present, no other substitute that might yield better results.

Some Muslim states are currently caught up in the conflict between Islamic forms of democracy. It is probably due to this reason that there are occasional instances of political breakdowns leading to military takeovers.

However, as has been pointed out, the fundamental principles on which an Islamic state is founded remain the same. A Muslim

national state can only claim to be an Islamic state when its constitution strictly adheres to the principles of Allah's ultimate
sovereignty and the supremacy of the shari'ah. Nevertheless, it
must be clearly understood that an Islamic state is not a theocracy.

Islam does not recognize the distinction between 'spiritual' and
'secular,' and every Muslim is required to constantly internalize
spiritual values while performing his temporal obligations. In this
sense, the Islamic state assimilates the qualities of an ideal secular state. In the positive sense, a secular state ought to guarantee religious freedom to every citizen and endeavor to promote
the material advancement and welfare of all its citizens irrespective of religion or race. This is also one of the duties of an Islamic
state, which at the same time must protect the places of worship
and culture of citizens who adhere to faiths other than Islam. The
Qur'an says: "If Allah had not raised a group [i.e., Muslims] to
ward off others from aggression, churches, synagogues, oratories
and mosques, [then, the places] where Allah is worshipped most
would have been destroyed." Since the faith and culture of religious minorities are to be protected, they can adopt any measure
of self-protection, including the demand for separate electorates
or representation in the form of a fixed quota of seats in the assembly.

In our time, there are numerous concepts of human rights
based on different ideologies. The capitalist democracies have
generated the concept of man having certain inalienable rights,
and place emphasis on the political and civil rights of an individual whereas the Marxist countries have forwarded the concept
of people's rights, with emphasis on the economic rights of a
group. There is also a concept of welfare rights advanced by
some countries which do not adhere to capitalist or Marxist
ideologies. In Islam, human rights are based on the faith itself. A
peculiar feature of Islam is that it conceives of two broad
categories of rights: those of Allah (*huququllah*) and those of men
(*huququl 'ibad*). The Islamic state, therefore, guarantees the rights
of Allah as well as those of men. The rights of men that can be
found in the Qur'an and Sunnah are those of life, asylum, individual freedom, equality before the law, justice, fair trial, protection of honor and reputation; protection against abuse of power,
against torture; equality of status and opportunity; freedom of
thought, expression, belief, faith, worship, association, assembly,
movement, trade, business or profession; to hold and dispose of
property; protection of minorities; to participate in the conduct and
management of public affairs; status and dignity of workers; social security, founding a family and related matters; of married

women; education or privacy; and so on, subject to Islamic law and morality. During the times of the rightly guided caliphs, the rights were known and upheld since everyone studied the Qur'an. This can be illustrated by an example. Islam allows no interference or intrusion into the personal or family affairs of anyone. Spying is forbidden except in times of war, especially when there is suspicion about a person being an enemy's agent. On the other hand, in normal times, even if there is a strong probability that something wrong is going on in someone's house, no warrant can be issued against him nor is there a justification to spy upon him. It is reported that one night while crossing a street of Medinah, Caliph 'Umar heard sounds of debauchery coming from inside a house. He lost his temper and tried to enter the house, but no one answered his knock at the door. He climbed upon the roof and from it shouted down to the owner who was present in his lawn: "Why are you breaking the law and allowing such behavior in your house?" The man replied: "No Muslim has the right to speak to another in that manner. Maybe I have committed a wrong, but think how many wrongs you have committed. For instance: (1) spying — despite Allah's command 'thou shalt not spy'; (2) breaking and entering — you came in over the roof despite the command of Allah, 'enter a house by the door'; (3) entering without the owner's permission — in defiance of Allah's command: 'enter no house without the owner's permission'; (4) omitting the *salām* — though Allah has commanded 'enter no house without indicating that you are a friend and calling peace (salām) on those within'." 'Umar felt very embarrassed and withdrew saying: "Well, I forgive your wrong." The owner retorted: "That is your fifth infringement; for if you claim to be an executor of Islamic law, then how can you say that you forgive what Allah has condemned as a wrong?"

This clearly illustrates how conscious every Muslim citizen of the early Islamic state was of his rights. For guaranteeing the rights of men, the Islamic state must ensure the complete independence of the judiciary, for this is the only way to uphold the supremacy of the Islamic law.

The legislature in an Islamic state has a restricted role; technically speaking, its authority is delegated and can be exercised only within the limits prescribed by the Qur'an and Sunnah. Therefore, it must enjoin what is considered by the Qur'an as *ma'ruf* (universally acknowledged moral values). According to some jurists, in certain exceptional cases a Qur'anic injunction can temporarily be suspended, a belief which is based upon 'Umar's suspension of the punishment (*hadd*) of cutting a thief's hand in the times of famine in Medinah. Similarly, permission granted by the Qur'an to a Muslim for marrying more than one wife can be temporarily suspended or withdrawn if it leads to adverse social results. Generally speaking, there are three possible spheres for legislative activity in a Muslim national state:

(1) to enforce laws which have specifically been laid down in the Qur'an and Sunnah,

(2) to bring all existing laws in conformity with the Qur'an and Sunnah, and

(3) to make laws as subordinate legislation which do not violate the Qur'an and Sunnah.

Establishing such a legislature through elections first of all requires an electorate which is aware of its rights and obligations under the Islamic law. Second, representatives must be elected either on a non-party basis or through those political parties which adhere to the Islamic ideology and are in a position to put up qualified candidates. Third, measures must be adopted which clearly determine which candidate has the overwhelming support of the voters.

A modern Muslim legislative assembly, at least for the present, would consist mostly of members who possess no knowledge of the subtleties of Islamic law. Therefore, they are likely to make errors in their interpretation of Islamic law. Ideally speaking, if an elected legislative assembly is formed in an Islamic state, it should consist of lawyers qualified in Islamic law and jurisprudence. This objective can be realized through a reform in the present system of legal education in Muslim countries by combining the study of Islamic law with an enlightened study of modern jurisprudence.

For the interim period, two constitutional devices have been adopted by some Muslim national states to reduce the possibility of erroneous interpretations of Islamic law. These are: making provisions within the assembly for a separate committee of scholars to supervise its legislative activity as an advisory council and to advise it on the law's compatibility, or lack thereof, with Islamic norms and concepts.

According to some modern Muslim jurists, the presidential form of democracy is closer to the Islamic concept of state, whereas others say that it makes little difference whether the form of democracy is presidential or parliamentary. The main point is acknowledging Allah's sovereignty by upholding the supremacy of Islamic law. As far as the enforcement of Islamic law is concerned, the Muslim community is at liberty to create any mode of constitutional structure which it deems suitable for its particular situation, as long as it is based on the principle of "mutual consultation."

THE CONTRACT FOR THE APPOINTMENT OF THE HEAD OF AN ISLAMIC STATE

Fathi Osman

Political thinkers have always been interested in limiting a ruler's authority in order to avoid its possible abuse. Not satisfied with defining a ruler's authority by means of ever-changing constitutional laws, present-day political thinkers have tried to restrict it at its source, thereby requiring the rulers to act within a specific legal framework.

The Social Contract in Western Thought

One of the most distinguished achievements in this field is the Social Contract theory formulated in the 17th and 18th centuries by John Locke (d. 1704) and Jean-Jacques Rousseau (d. 1778). The theory is based on the assumption that a contract was signed in the distant past between the leader of a given society and its people. This contract stipulated that the leader would use his authority to represent the will of all of his subjects, not just that of the majority. Consequently, any harm done by a ruler to any individual implied a violation of this elemental stipulation. Regardless of whether this violation was supported by a legislative or an administrative decision, neither could justify this breach of the social contract. Should such a decision be issued, it would have been considered void.

Equally, whether or not this theory ever came into existence has held no bearing on the practice of absolute rule or the emergence of other philosophies purporting such a system of government. Thomas Hobbs (d. 1679), writing earlier than Locke and Rousseau's essays, and Friedrich Hegel (d. 1831), whose work appeared later, both sought to support a ruler's absolute authority, arguing that the individual had surrendered all rights to the leader when accepting his leadership. Neither theory could be proven to have a majority among its supporters.

In the early days of Islam, a real — not merely hypothetical — contract was drawn up between the ruled and the rulers. After the death of the Prophet (11 A.H. / 632 C.E.), the first four caliphs held their offices as a result of a free election. The public agreement which gave the caliph his power is known as *bai'ah*, (from the root bai'ah, meaning 'to sell'). The Qur'anic principle of *shura* (counsel) inspired this unique historical experiment.

The original sources of Islam — the Qur'an and the Sunnah — provide limited legal texts in various fields. When exigency demands, new laws can be made through *ijtihad* — a process which develops new laws by employing juridical reasoning in the examination of the original text and previous cases. *Fiqh*, that enormous corpus of laws, is the product of this intellectual process. Ijtihad, however, is an unending process; thus, the fiqh of the past, valuable as it might be, is neither unchangeable nor infallible.[1]

Bai'ah in Historical Practice

Early Muslims responded to changing circumstances by following the Islamic principles as understood and lived by the companions of the Prophet. The juristic formulation and elaboration came later. Historically, the bai'ah of the first four caliphs (*ar-Rashidun*) took place in the years 11 A.H. (632 C.E.), 13 A.H. (634 C.E.), 23 A.H. (644 C.E.) and 35 A.H. (656 C.E.). In every case, the leading personalities of the Muslim community in Medinah talked about the nominees, made their decision, and then gave their bai'ah to the caliph in the mosque.[2] This early practice of the companions of the Prophet inspired later juristic works which sought to define and qualify the legal appointment of the ruler (imam), and the legal relations between him and his people.

Bai'ah in the Juristic Heritage

As jurisprudence developed, jurists viewed the bai'ah accorded to the first four caliphs as a mere contract. This was clear among

---

[1]The law of Islam (shari'ah), to the extent that it is based on the clear injunctions of the Qur'an and Sunnah, is permanent. However, the intellectual derivations represented in the voluminous jurisprudential works and the accumulated practice of the Muslim ummah during successive centuries are changeable. There is a tendency to ignore this basic distinction between these two parts of the shari'ah. See Muhammad Asad, *The Principles of State and Government in Islam* (Gibraltar: Dar al-Andalus, 1980), pp. 11-15; also, 'Abd al-Razzaq al-Sanhuri, "Nahwa Qanun Arabi Muwahadd" in *al-Thaqafa al-'Arabiyyah* (Cairo: n.p., 1951).

[2]For detailed historical reports about the appointment of each of the first four caliphs see, at-Tabari, *Tarikh ar-Rusul wa al-Muluk*, vols. 3-5 (Cairo: al-Husayniyyah Press, n.y.). For a brief survey, see: Hasan Ibrahim Hasan, *An-Nazum al-Islamiyyah*; Syed Ameer Ali, *A Short History of the Saracens*; and Thomas Arnold, *The Caliphate*.

the sunnis, who did not accept the shi'ite claim that the Prophet had nominated 'Ali ibn Abi Talib and his descendants as successive imams after his death. In their argument against the shi'ite claim, sunni theologians and jurists emphasized that the appointment of the imam is a prerogative of the ummah (*ikhtiyar al-ummah*), and thus the claim of divine nomination formulated by the shi'ite theologians is not tenable. The subject of imamate formed an integral part of theological works, as various Muslim doctrines (sunni, shi'ite and khariji) came into being mainly because of the differing views of their adherents concerning the imamate.[3]

Works attacking shi'ite ideas, such as those of al-Baqillani (d. 403 A.H. / 1013 C.E.) and Ibn Taimiyyah (d. 718 A.H. / 1328 C.E.)[4], provide good examples. After a lengthy refutation of the shi'ite claim of the imam's divine nomination, al-Baqillani said: "The imam holds his office because of a contract drawn by the wise (ahl al-hall wa al-'aqd) ..." To al-Baqillani any claimed tradition (of the Prophet) or any interpretation of a tradition about a divine nomination of a certain imam is false, for an imam can only be appointed through the choice of the people (*al-ikhtiyar*). Ibn Khaldun (d. 808 A.H. / 1406 C.E.) as well as others stated that the public duty of choosing an imam can be supported by the legal evidence of consensus (*ijma*)[5].

The expression "the contract for the appointment of the imam, *'aqd al-imamah*" was used frequently by sunni theologians and jurists. The imam is the result of a contract "*ma'qud lahu*" — he does not enjoy any metaphysical or theocratic privilege, and the contract can be dissolved when he loses the essential qualifications for his position. The Zaydis, a shi'ite sub-group, believe that the imam should be chosen from the descendants of 'Ali and Fatimah, for only 'Ali was personally appointed by a revealed tradition. The one selected should enjoy the legal status of an imam, including a public proclamation of his imamate and his opposition to any ruler considered by the Zaydis to be an usurper of authority.[6] However, the Ithna 'ashri or Ja'fari shi'ites have

---

[3]See for example: al-Baqillani, *at-Tamhid*; al-Baghdadi, *Usul al-Din*; al-Juwayni, *al-Irshad*; al-Mawardi, *al-Ahkam as-Sultaniyyah*; and Abu Ya'la, *al-Ahkam as-Sultaniyyah*.

[4]Their works were (in Arabic): *at-Tamhid fi ar-Radd 'ala al-Mulhida...*, and *Minhaj as-Sunnah*.

[5]Ibn Khaldun, *al-Muqaddimah* (Beirut: Dar al-Qalam, 1978), pp. 191-2; but compare: al-Mawardi, *al-Ahkam as-Sultaniyyah* (Beirut: n.p., 1978), p.5.

[6]Ibn Khaldun, pp. 197-98.

practically accepted a deputy for the imam after the disappearance of the last imam, provided that he is chosen in accordance
with Islamic law.[7]

These statements indicate that previous Muslim jurists identified
the public contract as a means to appoint the imam. Al-Sanhuri,
a contemporary Egyptian lawyer, has stated that the imam's appointment (in accordance with historical practice and as formulated and elaborated in juristic literature) represented a real contract which sought to designate the imam or the caliph for the
Muslim state. He also points out that the imam's authority is derived from his contract with the Muslim people.[8]

Al-Baqillani, the well-known theologian, stated in his *at-Tamhid*
that the imam is a procurator and representative of the people,
who must support him and remind him of his duties and responsibilities as well as force him to follow the right way. If he persists
in wrongdoing, the people may depose him and replace him with
someone else as a last resort.[9] The characterization of the imamate as a public procurement was repeated in many theological
and juridicial works.[10] Since the appointment of the first caliph
(Abu Bakr) and his first public speech, this principle has been
clearly stated. He said: "I have been appointed as your ruler, and
I am not the best of you. If you find me following the right way,
support me. If not, correct me. Obey me as long as I obey Allah;
if I disobey Him, my obedience is not binding upon you." A significant comment on this statement was reported from Imam Malik
— the founder of the Maliki juristic school (d. 179 A.H. / 795 C.E.)
— who observed that what Abu Bakr mentioned is an essential
condition for the appointment of any imam.[11] The first caliph's
statement indicates the imam's responsibility in following the
teachings of Islam, as well as the fact that he is appointed,
watched and corrected by the people. Al-Kasani, the distinguished Hanafi jurist (d. 587H. / 1191 C.E.), in his voluminous

---

[7]al-Khomeini, *al-Hukuma al-Islamiyyah* (Beirut), pp. 23 seq.; see also, Diya' ad-Din
ar-Rayyis, *an-Nazariyyat as-Siyasiyyah al-Islamiyyah* (Cairo: n.p., 1951), p. 167.

[8]As-Sanhury: *Le Califat* (Paris: n.p., 1926), pp. 5, 17-19, 94.

[9]Al-Baqillani, *at-Tamhid* in the selections of Y. Ibish, *Nusus al-Fikr as-Siyasi al-Islami, al-Imama 'ind as-Sunna* (Beirut: n.p., 1966), p. 56.

[10]See, for example, a selection from Abu Ya'la, the theologian and Hanbali jurist,
in his work, *al-Mu'tamad fi Usul ad-Din*, by Ibish, *Ibid.*, p. 213; and Ibn
Taimiyyah, *as-Siyasa ash-Shar'iyyah* (Cairo: n.p., 1969), p. 13.

[11]Reported by as-Suyuti and quoted by Rafiq al-Azm, *Ashhar Mashahir al-Islam*,
vol. 1, the section on Abu Bakr's speeches.

work *al-Bada'i* suggests that a judge is a procurator of the supreme ruler — the caliph — in the administration of justice, but
when a caliph dies, the judges keep their positions "because a
judge is really appointed by the Muslim people to work for them,
and a caliph represents merely one who carries the public mes-
sage to the concerned ..."[12] Therefore, a judge keeps his position
and exercises his authority even after the caliph's death, because
the people who represent the real source of his authority continue
to exist whatever happens to the caliph. This concept was also
clarified and elaborated on by al-Mawardi, the Shaf'i jurist (d.
450 H. / 1058 C.E.), in his work *Adal al-Qadi*;[13] and by other legal
scholars. Some jurists suggest that the imam cannot depose a
judge as long as he carries out his function rightfully, since he
does not work for the imam but rather the whole Muslim people,
and takes care of their interests.[14] In addition to the imam being
a procurator and a representative of the people, some 'ulema
noticed that certain responsibilities, such as the defense of the
faith and the land, cannot be fulfilled except through a full cooperation between the leader and his followers.[15] In fact, the imam
cannot perform his responsibilities efficiently if the people remain
passive. It is the right of the ruler and the duty of the ruled to
support and cooperate with the ruler as long as he practices his
authority in the right way.[16] The people, while they are judging
the imam's policies, should support what they agree with and oppose what they do not like.

The Legal Qualification of the Imamate Contract

Works on the fundamentals of Islamic jurisprudence, *usul al-fiqh*
make a distinction between injunctions and prohibitions – that is,
the right of God and the right of people (*haqq al-'ibad*). The right
of God refers to what is beneficial for the people, and thus, it cannot

---

[12]Muhammad ash-Shaf'i al-Labban, "Mabda Siyadat al-Ummat fi al-Fiqh al-Islami," in *al-Fajr as-Sadiq*, vol. V, 1948.

[13]Al-Mawardi, *Adab al-Qadi*, vol. 2, ed. Muhyi Hilal Sarhan, (Baghdad: n.p.,
1971), pp. 142, 399; see also a brief statement in his general work: *al-Ahkam as-
Sultaniyyah*, p. 70.

[14]Abu Ya'la, *al-Ahkam as-Sultaniyyah*, ed. Hamid al-Faqi (Cairo: n.p., 1974), p.
65.

[15]'Abd al-Jabbar, *al-Mughni*, vol. 20 (Cairo: n.p., n.d.), part II, p. 163.

[16]Abu Ya'la, *al-Ahkam as-Sultaniyyah*, p. 28; see also, Al-Mawardi, *al-Ahkam as-
Sultaniyyah*, p. 17.

be related to any particular individual or group.[17] From this, present-day jurists have drawn that the right of God also includes sha'a'ir al-'ibadah – rules which relate to the public benefit.[18] However, the right of God, as ash-Shatibi (d. 790 A.H. / 1389 C.E.) pointed out in his distinguished work on usul al-Muwafaqat, cannot be excluded from any rule that deals with the right of the individual, since the individual's right is protected by the divine law, which has to be obeyed. A third category was mentioned for the rules in which both the right of God and the right of the people are observed together, as in the case of penalties for certain crimes.[19] The contract of imamate was included in this last category.[20]

Sometimes the imam has been characterized in hadith and in the juristic works as God's agent who takes care of His servants.[21] This should be understood as an emphasis on the responsibility of the ruler toward God, without any theocratic privilege. The public choice of the imam, along with the assurance of mutual rights and duties of the ruled and the ruler were called bai'ah – a derivative from a root that means 'to sell.' The Qur'an uses this term[22] for the promise given to the Prophet by the early Muslims to observe the Islamic teachings and obey the Prophet. This was spelled out while the believer was putting his hand in that of the prophet. Ibn Khaldun says (d. 808 A.H. / 1406 C.E.) that "when Muslims extended their bai'ah to the ruler and gave him their promise of obedience, they put their hands in his hand, something which was similar to the act of the seller and the buyer." This holding of hands became a symbol of bai'ah.

Ibn Khaldun considers bai'ah to be a promise of public obedience to the ruler.[23] In fact, bai'ah represents the transfer of public authority to the imam and the imam's promise to observe Islamic law and fulfill the expectations of the public. Etymologically, the

---

[17]See for example, at-Taftanzani, Hashiyat at-Talwih 'ala at-Tawdih by Sadr ash-Shari'ah, vol. 2 (Cairo: n.p., 1327 A.H.), p. 140.

[18]'Abd al-Wahhab Khallaf, 'Ilm Usul al-Fiqh, 8th edition (Kuwait: n.p., 1968), pp. 210-11.

[19]Ash-Shatibi, al-Muwafaqat, vol.2, commented on by 'Abd Allah Diraz (Cairo: n.p., n.d.), pp. 315 seq., especially pp. 322-323.

[20]Al-Mawardi, al-Ahkam as-Sultaniyyah, p. 8.

[21]See for example: Ibn Taimiyyah, as-Siyasah ash-Shar'iyyah (Cairo: n.p., n.d.), pp. 11-13.

[22]See the Qur'an 9:3, 3:10,18, 60:12. For the bai'ah of 'Aqaba and the bai'ah of the Tree, see Ibn Hisham, Sirat an-Nabi, vol. 3.

[23]Ibn Khaldun, al-Muqaddimah p. 209.

verb bai'ah expresses an act undertaken by both parties, resulting in mutual obligations. Commenting on bai'ah, Abu Ya'la says
it is given on the condition that the imam observes justice and
fulfills the responsibilities of his position. Thus, bai'ah is not only
the obligation of the ruled to obey the ruler, but also their conditions for obedience. As soon as the ruler accepts the conditions
of the ruled, they become his obligations. Moreover, Abu Ya'la
emphasizes that the cornerstone of this contract is the expression
of satisfaction on the part of the people who give the bai'ah, be
it in words or another form. Therefore, no formal statement or action of holding hands is required; the content of the contract can
be expressed in any way.[24]

Ibn Taimiyyah emphasizes that the authority which a ruler enjoys is a responsibility and should be fulfilled honestly. In his
opinion, it is similar to the responsibilities of an orphan's tutor, an
endowment funds trustee and someone's procurator. A ruler
should take care of his people, as a shepherd does of his flock.
He is hired by his people to work for their benefit. In this way,
the contract represents some elements of tutorship, employment,
and procurement all combined together.[25] In any case, the rights
of the other party — the minor, the employer, or the procurer —
come first and foremost. Ibn Taimiyyah delineates the mutual obligations of both parties, thereby turning the contract into a form
of partnership.[26] This characterizes the rights and obligations of
both parties in a balanced way because people may be short-
sighted or passive, demanding rights without taking responsibilities.

No matter how similar the contract of imamate may appear to
any other contract, Muslim jurists are quite aware of the differences between contracts of public and private interests in their
legal nature and effects. It has been mentioned elsewhere that
al-Kasani, as well as al-Mawardi, Abu Ya'la and others, pointed
out how different any private procurement was from the legal
situation of a judge who works in the administration of justice as
the imam's procurator, when in fact, he is the public procurator
in his function. Al-Mawardi also says that flexibility is required
when accepting the nomination of several successors for the
caliphate. They would follow one after another, as distinct from

---

[24]Abu Ya'la, *al-Ahkam as-Sultaniyyah*, p. 25; see also: *al-Mu'tamad*, in the selections of Ibish, *Nusua*, p. 224.

[25]Ibn Taimiyyah, *as-Siyasah ash-Shar'iyyah*, pp. 11-12.

[26]*Ibid*, p. 13.

any other contract of guardianship on the grounds of "public interest which should be seen in a wider perspective than private contracts."[27] Comparing the *kharaj* levied by Caliph 'Umar ibn al-Khattab on the conquered lands with the land rent, the Hanbaliyyah jurists Ibn 'Aqil and Ibn Taimiyyah state that the kharaj should be understood as a specific act (sui generis) and akin to a contract, based on the consideration of the general interests of the people and their faith. Sometimes the conquered land was classified as *waqf* which, as clarified by Ibn Rajab, should not be taken literally nor should it have the legal implications of a private waqf.[28]

The Public Party in the Contract of Bai'ah

If the imam is appointed by a public contract as the historical practice and juristic heritage clearly indicates, who is the other party? How would the people be represented?

According to the historical practice of the early caliphate, some leading persons gave their bai'ah after discussion. The bai'ah of that limited circle was followed by the bai'ah of the masses, which the caliph received in the mosque. Some historians may call the decision of the leading persons a special bai'ah or a bai'ah of the special.[29] In juristic literature, they are known as *ahl al-hall wa al-'aqd* (those who are eligible to bind and dissolve – that is, make decisions).[30]

The selection of an imam is considered by the jurists to be a social or collective duty (*fard kifayah*) for which the Muslim people as a whole are responsible as they are for service, learning of specific knowledge, teaching, or sitting as a judge. As for the individual duty (*fard 'ayn*), such as the performance of the daily prayers, fasting, or the payment of *zakah*, every Muslim adult is held personally accountable. Al-Mawardi indicates that the selectors of the imam should enjoy testimonial acceptability (according to the rulers of *'adalah*), knowledge of the requirements of the position, and the wisdom which enables them to

---

[27]Al-Mawardi, *al-Ahkam as-Sultaniyyah*, p. 13. For other examples of al-Mawardi's differentiation between public and private legal acts, see pp. 9, 24.

[28]Ibn Rajab, *al-Istikhraj fi Ahkam al-Kharaj* (Cairo: n.p., 1352 A.H.), pp. 40, 49, 97.

[29]See for example, Hasan Ibrahim Hasan and 'Ali Ibrahim, *An-Nazum al-Islamiyyah*.

[30]The term may also be mentioned as *ahl al-hall wa al-'aqd*, to stress their authority of dissolving and annulling, but it seems more reasonable to the present writer to begin by stressing the authority of binding.

select the most capable person for the post.[31]

Only a general description of the qualities of "ahl al-hall wa al-'aqd" or *ahl al-ikhtiyar* can be found in the juristic literature. The first two caliphs assumed the leadership of the Muslims after a discussion among the leading companions of the Prophet in Medinah, the capital of the new Islamic state. When the second caliph, 'Umar, was assassinated, the caliphate had already become a universal state, and the leading companions of the Prophet had dispersed throughout the conquered lands. 'Umar nominated six persons for the caliphate and asked them to choose one among themselves. Even so, this did not mean that the "ahl hall wa al-'aqd" at that time were restricted to those six persons only. One of them, 'Abd ar-Rahman ibn 'Awf, withdrew his name and undertook the responsibility of discussing the matter with the remaining candidates as well as with other leading persons in Medinah. Some of them who lived away from Medinah came to the city as soon as they heard of the death of the caliph. Even that spontaneous reaction did not represent any deliberate decision of the central administration to call into session those who might be defined as eligible at that time to elect the caliph. This was also the situation when the third caliph, 'Uthman, was killed and 'Ali ibn Abi Talib was chosen to succeed him.

By the time the Umayyad dynasty had entrenched itself, the Islamic state — or the several states in later times — came under the domination of absolute monarchic dynasties or military authorities. In these circumstances, no administrative procedure was considered necessary to define the "ahl al-hall wa al-'aqd" because the successor was chosen by the incumbent ruler after consulting the elders of the monarchic family or the senior army officers. However, the term "ahl al-hall wa al-'aqd" survives in our juristic heritage in spite of its vagueness and impractibility. Some commentators on the Qur'an explained that the public obedience required in an-Nisa': 59 should apply to those who are eligible for binding and dissolving in general and is not restricted to the existing rulers. The verse reads: "O you who have attained faith, obey Allah and obey the Messenger and those from among you who have been entrusted with authority. If you are at variance over any matter, refer it unto Allah and the Messenger if you truly believe in Allah and the Last Day." It indicates that persons in authority should be *entrusted with it*; this necessarily implies a free decision by the people to select their ruler (from among them-

---

[31] Al-Mawardi, *al-Ahkam as-Sultaiyyah*, p. 6; see also: Abu Ya'la, *al-Ahkam as-Sultaniyyah*, p. 19.

selves). While some commentators believed that the authorities (ulu'l-'amr) to be obeyed in accordance with the preceding verse are the rulers or the scholars of religion others understood it to include both the rulers and scholars.[32] A later commentator, al-Nisaburi, explained that the term ulu'l-'amr actually meant "ahl al-hall wa al-'aqd." This view has also been supported by the Egyptian reformer Muhammad 'Abdu (d. 1905),[33] who was more inclined to restrict the authority of the rulers by considering the shura as the basic authority in the Muslim community and the Islamic state. The verse makes it absolutely clear that the ruler's authority is not absolute and that disputes over public decisions must be settled with reference to the Qur'an and Sunnah. This is also clear from the linguistic structure of the verse and was explained on semantic grounds by the distinguished Hanbaliyyah jurist Ibn al-Qayyim (d. 751 A.H. / 1350 C.E.), the brilliant disciple of Ibn Taimiyyah.[34]

Muhammad 'Abdu tried to delineate the various components of "ahl al-hall wa al-'aqd." The shura as a body in Sheikh 'Abdu's words consists of: the supreme rulers (al-umara); the rulers (al-hukkam) — a term which may include central and local rulers, administrative and judicial authorities, and so on); scholars ('ulema); the military chiefs; and "all other chiefs and leaders from whom the people seek help and support when they need something." The last component appears to include the same people whom al-Nisaburi called "those of distinguished ranks and considerable opinions."[35] An-Nawawi (d. 676 A.H. / 1279 C.E.), in al-Minhaj, defined "ahl al hall wa al-'aqd" as "the leaders and the distinguished among the people."[36]

Later, Hasan al-Banna (d. 1949), the founder of Egypt's Muslim Brotherhood, stated that the qualities of "ahl al-hall wa al-'aqd," according to the juristic elaboration, can be applied to three groups: jurists capable of discovering solutions to emerging problems in light of the legal methods of ijtihad; experienced people in public affairs; and those "who practice a kind of leadership

---

[32]See Ibn Kathir, Tafsir, Volume 1; al-Qurtubi, Tafsir, volume 5 - commenting on this verse in an-Nisa':59; also: Ibn Taimiyyah, as-Siyasah ash-Shari'yyah, p. 159.

[33]Muhammad 'Abdu, Muhammad Rashid Rida, Tafsir al-Manar,vol 5 (Cairo: n.p., n.d.), pp. 181-183.

[34]Ibn al-Qayyim, I'lam al-Muwaqi'in, vol. 1 (Cairo: al-Muniriyya Press, n.d.), p. 39.

[35]Muhammad 'Abdu, Tafsir al-Manar, vol. 5 (Cairo: n.p., n.d.), pp. 181-183.

[36]Quoted by ar-Rayyis in an-Nazariyyat as-Siyasiyyah, p. 179.

among people as heads of families, tribes, or groups."[37] This list restricts 'ulema to those who are capable of using ijtihad to perform their legislative functions, a condition which may comply with al-Baghdadi's term *ahl al-ijtihad* in his work *Usul ud-Din*[38] and with the other term *ahl al-ijma'* (those whose views can be counted in a consensus) which was mentioned by the commentator al-Nisaburi and his predecessor al-Fakhr al-Razi (d. 606 A.H. / 1209 C.E.).[39] According to al-Banna, the official 'ulema, such as those related to *al-Azhar* establishment, may be excluded since they never practice ijtihad, have no independent thinking, and merely follow the directions of the government. In contrast to Sheikh 'Abdu, al-Banna does not include the military chiefs but rather identifies this leadership as mainly social (heads of families and tribes) and not governmental. The expression 'chiefs of groups' is very vague in al-Banna's list. It may refer to trade unions, which have existed in Egypt since the Middle Ages and find their counterparts today in unions of workers and professionals. Moreover, al-Banna might include the leaders of popular ideological or religious associations, such as the Muslim Brotherhood. It is difficult to decide whether non-Muslim sectarian or social bodies are included in "ahl al hall wa al-'aqd" or not. Since al-Banna was opposed to the existence of political parties in an Islamic state, one should assume that he would exclude them from his shura body.[40]

It is obvious from the preceding discussion that many questions still remain unresolved. As a contemporary Egyptian scholar points, the precedent of Caliph 'Umar in nominating a shura body to chose the next caliph remains unique in the history of Islam since it was neither followed in later political practice nor was it developed theoretically in juristic literature.[41]

Abu Ya'la rejects the idea of the imam nominating the "ahl al-hall wa al-'aqd."[42]

The Quorum Required for Bai'ah

Both the definition of shura and a quorum of the " ahl al-hall

---

[37]Hasan al-Banna, "Mushkilatuna fi Da'wa an-Nizam al-Islami" in *Majmu' ar-Rasa'il al-Imam ash-Shaheed Hasan al-Banna* (Beirut: n.p., n.d.), p. 377.

[38]Quoted by ar-Rayyis in *an-Nazariyyat as-Siyassiyyah*, p. 181.

[39]*Tafsir al-Manar*, Volume V, pp. 182-183.

[40]See for example al-Banna, loc. cit., pp. 105, 192, 372-6.

[41]Al-Khudari, *Muhadarat Tarikh al-'Umam al-Islamiyyah*, vol. 1, part 1 and 2.

[42]Abu Ya'la, *al-Ahkam as-Sultaniyyah*, p. 26.

wa al-'aqd," which could make a binding decision, remained vague in historical practice and juristic literature. For this reason, many different opinions on these two issues arose among jurists. While some jurists devised a certain quorum for making a binding decision on the imam's bai'ah, many others did not do so and believed that any number of the "ahl al-hall wa al-'aqd" — even a single person — could carry out the bai'ah, as long as it was accepted by others. Abu Ya'la states that the agreement of the whole or of a considerable majority of the "ahl al-hall wa al-'aqd" for the bai'ah was the most obvious and prevalent view in the Hanbali school.[43]

The jurists who stipulated a quorum of the "ahl al-hall wa al-'aqd" for the imam's bai'ah mention a certain number: five, three, and forty. The first figure was based on the historical precedent of the earliest participants in the bai'ah of Abu Bakr.[44] It was also supported by the number of participants who formed the majority among the six nominated by 'Umar to choose his successor.[45] The number of those who took the initiative in the bai'ah of Abu Bakr provided a very weak support for this opinion, while the case of shura about 'Umar's successor provided no support at all since the bai'ah could be decided only by four according to the procedure laid down by 'Umar. For the quorum of three persons, it was assumed that the bai'ah might be similar to a decision of a judge based on the testimony of two, or of a marriage contract settled by the father or guardian of the bride in addition to two witnesses.[46] This argument is not convincing since there is a clear difference between these cases. The situation of a judge is different from that of a witness, and both are different from the case of a participant in the bai'ah. In addition, a marriage contract is completely different from the bai'ah. The suggestion for a quorum of forty people was based on the minimum number (forty) of people needed to perform the Friday prayer.[47] However, this is also not entirely relevant to bai'ah.

The bai'ah is, however, binding, irrespective of the number of "ahl al-hall wa al-'aqd" who participate in it. This has been the

---

[43]*Ibid.*, pp. 23-24; see also his *al-Mu'tamad* in Ibish, *Nusus*, pp. 212-213.

[44]They were 'Umar, Abu 'Ubaydah, Usayd ibn Hudayr, Bashir ibn Sa'd, and Salim, the *mawla* (protege') of Abu Hudhayfah. See al-Mawardi, *al-Ahkam as-Sultanfyyah*, p. 7.

[45]*Ibid.*

[46]*Ibid.*

[47]Ar-Rayyis, *an-Nazariyyat as-Siyasiyyah*, p. 182.

opinion of many prominent theologians such as al-Ash'ari (d. 330 A.H. / 942 C.E.), al-Baqillani, al-Qalanisi, al-Baghdadi, al-Ghazzali, al-Juwayni (d. 478 A.H. / 1085 C.E.), and al-Shihristani (d. 548 A.H. / 1153 C.E.), as well as many jurists.[48] Some of them stipulated that any number of witnesses could attend the imam's bai'ah.[49]

It was assumed by theologians and jurists that the person who might settle the bai'ah for an imam should necessarily represent all of "ahl al-hall wa al-'aqd." Al-Ghazzali and Ibn Taimiyyah argue that Abu Bakr's nomination of 'Umar as his successor could only be considered a bai'ah of imam if those who were eligible for binding and dissolving agreed to accept him as their leader.[50] Al-Ghazzali explains that the one among "ahl al-hall wa al-'aqd" whose bai'ah for the imam could be considered as binding was the person who enjoyed high power (*shawkah*) and had massive public support. The bai'ah of such a person would be effective as long as he is followed and obeyed by the masses, and his authority cannot be overruled by those who may differ with him, for they lack comparable social and political weight. The purpose of bai'ah is to provide the imam with public support; those who can secure this support in his behalf are eligible to make the binding decision regardless of their number. If these qualities are enjoyed by more than one person, they should agree about the bai'ah because a decision by only one of them would not be publicly binding.[51] Ibn Taimiyyah repeats the argument of al-Ghazzali, emphasizing that an imam cannot practice his authority unless he is supported by those who enjoy power (ahl al-shawkah). Such authority cannot be secured by the approval of one or more persons unless public support can be secured.[52] While al-Ghazzali is realistic enough to assume the probable existence of some who may disagree with the bai'ah, he gives no weight to such an ineffective opposition. Al-Shihristani accepts the legitimacy of one-man bai'ah only when others in the group of "ahl hall wa al-

---

[48]See for example, Ibish, *Nusus*, pp. 48 49, 132-133, 150, 278, 313, 365; also ar-Rayyis, *an-Nazariyyat as-Siyasiyyah* pp. 181-82.

[49]See for example, the statements of al-Baqillani and al-Juwayrii in Ibish, *Nusus*, pp. 49, 278-279.

[50]Al-Ghazzali, *Fada'ih al-Batiniyyah*, quoted in Ibish, *Nusus*, p. 314; Ibn Taimiyyah, *Minhaj as-Sunnah an-Nabawiyyah*, vol. 1, 1st ed. (Cairo: n.p., 1321 A.H.), pp. 141-142.

[51]Al-Ghazzali in ibish's *Nusus*, loc. cit., pp. 313-314; also: *al-Iqtisad fi al-I'tiqad*, in *ibid*, pp. 365-366.

[52]Ibn Taimiyyah, *Minhaj as-Sunnah an-Nabawiyyah*, vol. 1, p. 141.

'aqd" do not openly express their opposition.[53]

Other safeguards could also be provided by juristic requirements for "ahl al-hall wa al-'aqd." As has been previously mentioned, al-Mawardi and Abu Ya'la required three qualifications for everyone in the shura: testimonial acceptability (al-'adalah), observance of Islam being the main component; legal knowledge; and wisdom in opinion and choice. Al-Baghdadi mentions two qualities: ability to perform ijtihad, and piety. If one of them is missing, the bai'ah cannot be carried out.[54] On the other hand, no bai'ah would be considered binding unless the candidate himself fulfills the requirements for the imamate. Al-Mawardi mentions five main qualities required for an imam: testimonial acceptability, the legal knowledge which enables him to practice ijtihad, physical fitness, wisdom, and courage. He adds that the imam must be related to the tribe of Quraysh.[55] Ibn Khaldun rejects the last requirement on the grounds that the imam should enjoy a communal support (asabiyyah), which was represented by the tribal unity of the Arabian sociopolitical structure. The tribe of Quraysh had enjoyed superiority among other Arab tribes during both the pre-Islamic period and the early centuries of Islam. Since sociopolitical power is temporary, any group which enjoys power and represents the communal asabiyyah at any given time would prevail in seizing the authority. Ibn Khaldun, therefore, believed that the imam's sociopolitical status should also be included in the list of necessary qualifications; yet, he tied it to the general requirement of 'capability,' along with three other requirements: religious knowledge, testimonial acceptability, and physical fitness.[56] According to him, the process of bai'ah must observe these three qualities in the candidate for imamate, otherwise it would be legally void — even if conducted by eligible persons.[57] Al-Mawardi emphasized that the bai'ah should be settled in favor of the most meritorious and capable one, "one to whom people would not hesitate to offer bai'ah and obedience."[58]

However, these juristic requirements were merely of theoretical nature. The jurists were aware of the fact that those who had the

---

[53]Quoted by ar-Rayyis in *an-Nuzariyyat as-Siyasiyyah*, p. 186.

[54]Ibish, *Nusus*, pp. 132-133.

[55]Al-Mawardi, *al-Ahkam as-Sultaniyyah*, p. 6, but compare with Abu Ya'la, *al-Ahkam as-Sultaniyyah*, p. 20.

[56]Ibn Khaldun, *al-Muqaddimah*, pp. 193-196.

[57]As reported by al-Baghdadi, this was also clearly stated by al-Ash'ari; see Ibish, *Nusus*, pp. 132-133.

[58]Al-Mawardi, *al-Ahkam as--Sultaniyyah*, p. 7.

power to appoint an imam did not actually fulfill the requirements for "ahl al-hall wa al-'aqd," especially in later times. The imams or the supreme rulers were themselves in the same boat. They felt that they should take the existing realities into account, even though they were far from the teachings of Islam ('umum al-balwa, as it was expressed by Hanafi jurists), and that they should observe the imperatives of public interest (al-Maslaha). Although they argued against the shi'ite claim of the imam's divine nomination and defended the public choice, they also realized that the concept of public choice in its true sense could hardly survive after the first four caliphs. The dilemma before the sunni jurists was that they could neither compromise on their normative theory, nor face the consequences of declaring the present authorities usurpers.

Ibn Khaldun endeavors to explain in his theory of asabiyyah that Mu'awiyah, the Umayyads in general, and the early 'Abbassids represented the dominant sociopolitical powers.[59] This explanation does seem plausible in some respects, but it fails to account for the use of continuous force by the authorities to suppress the contending forces. This formulation also fails to explain the large-scale disturbances that took place when the ruling authority was theoretically supposed to enjoy the superiority of asabiyyah. Ibn Khaldun's theory may explain the mechanism of the tribal forces among the Arabs before Islam and in early Islamic times, but it cannot apply to the complex relations among different ethnic groups and cultures in a universal state like the Islamic caliphate. After a lengthy argument, Ibn Khaldun admits that under the later Marwanids and the later 'Abbassids, Muslims came to be ruled by royal dynasties far removed from the teachings of Islam and the specific concepts of its polity.[60]

Al-Ghazzali has a more realistic approach in legitimizing the bai'ah of one or a few powerful people and the appointment of an imam who might lack some of the necessary qualifications for his position. He says such flexibility was temporary and meant to fulfill the needs of his time. In order to do that, he used the legal principle of maslaha, – that is, what is prohibited may be permitted if required by the public interest. Muslims need a ruler to defend the land, maintain security, punish offenders, carry out family law, ensure civil and commercial transactions, and appoint judges, even if such a ruler does not fulfill the juristic requirements for his function.[61] It was in view of these needs that al-

---

[59]Ibn Khaldun, *al-Muqaddimah, pp. 205-208.*

[60]*Ibid.*, p. 208.

[61]Al-Ghazzali, *al-Iqtisad*, in Ibish, *Nusus*, pp. 266-267.

Ghazzali, as well as other jurists, accepted the de facto authority of military rulers who seized power through force (al-ghalabah). This will be discussed in more detail later in this paper. Ibn Taimiyyah maintains that if an ideal ruler or public official could not be found, the one most suitable for the job should be appointed. However, Ibn Taimiyyah clearly stated that this was only a temporary device and that the Muslims must try to improve their conditions so they can comply with the teachings of Islam.[62]

Abu Ya'la, on the other hand, believes that a majority (jumhur) of the "ahl al-hall wa al-'aqd" should participate in the bai'ah of the imam since it was just as important as any other legal issue that calls for ijma'.[63] Some other theologians have also supported this view,[64] especially in the case of 'Ali ibn Abi Talib's caliphate. They argue that many companions of the Prophet were dispersed in different regions, and hence were unable to attend 'Ali's bai'ah in Medinah after the assassination of 'Uthman.[65] Al-Baqillani, in his argument for accepting any number of "ahl al-hall wa al-'aqd" for abai'ah, says it would be impossible to arrange a meeting of all such people because of the great distances involved. It would also be very difficult to arrive at a consensus among such a large number of people.[66] These practical considerations formed the basis for dropping the requirement of participation of a majority of the shura body in the bai'ah of the imam. This was clearly stated by an-Nawawi al-Minhaj, where he argues that the participation of the eligible people who could be easily gathered was acceptable.[67] Most of these arguments about the impractibility of getting people from all over the Islamic realm at one place seem irrelevant today. Developments in transportation and communication have made it possible to hold any number of such meetings. As for the argument about consensus, this may not be considered an absolute requirement, and a decision reached by a reasonable majority may be deemed sufficient.

Even though the bai'ah is a collective duty, it does not neces-

---

[62]Ibn Taimiyyah, as-Siyassah ash-Shar'iyyah pp. 13-21.

[63]Abu Ya'la, al-Mu'tamad in Ibish, Nusus, p. 24; also al-Ahkam as-Sultaniyyah, pp. 23-24.

[64]For the opinions of Abu Bakr al-Asam and Hisham ibn 'Amir al-Fuwati, who were both Mu'tazilites, see al-Mawardi al-Ahkam as-Sultaniyyah, p. 5. However, another Mu'tazilite, al-Jubba'i, believed that five would be a quorum for the bai'ah.

[65]Ibn Khaldun, al-Muqaddimah, p. 214.

[66]Al-Baqillani, at-Tamhid in Ibish, Nusus, p. 49.

[67]Quoted by ar-Rayyis, an-Nazariyyat as-Siyasiyyah, p. 179.

sarily imply that any number of "ahl al-hall wa al- 'aqd" may be sufficient in settling it. A reasonable number of Muslims, and not necessarily the whole community, has to come forward and participate in the process. An eligible Muslim is, however, individually responsible for participating in the discussion and decisions of the shura. We may also note that a juristic view considers the acceptanc of the imamate as binding on all (*fard 'ayn*) as soon as the imam receives the bai'ah, while the candidacy for the imamate is only fard kifayah.[68]

The Role of the Public Bai'ah

Historical sources report that the first four caliphs, after receiving the bai'ah of the ahl al-ikhtiyar or "ahl al-hall wa al-'aqd," attended public meetings in the mosque where the masses offered their bai'ah to them.[69] It is important to clarify the legal role of the public bai'ah and to determine whether it was binding for the legitimacy of their rule or if it was merely a ceremonial gesture.

This question, however, cannot be answered in any definitive manner. Historical sources do not mention any case of public opposition to the bai'ah of the first four caliphs once the decision had been reached by ahl-al-ikhtiyar. Opposition to 'Uthman was expressed several years after his bai'ah, but this was due to his policies, not to his appointment. The opponents of 'Ali maintained that many of the ahl al-ikhtiyar — represented at that time mainly by the companions of the Prophet — did not participate in his bai'ah; therefore, this also cannot be seen as public opposition against the decision of the ahl al-ikhtiyar. Some jurists, however, refer to the bai'ah of the people. Al-Mawardi, for example, argues that in their discussion on the choice of the imam, the "ahl al-hall wa al-'aqd" have to consider the chances of their candidate's endorsement by the people at large.[70] However, it is clear from the context that the bai'ah of ahl al-ikhtiyar is what actually counts for the bai'ah of an imam. Al-Mawardi also mentions that as soon as ahl al-ikhtiyar come to a decision about a candidate for the imamate, and he accepts the position, it becomes obligatory for the people to offer him their bai'ah and obey him.[71] Al-Mawardi

---

[68]Abu Ya'la, *al-Mu'tamad*, in Ibish, Nusus, pp. 213-214; *al-Ahkam as-Sultaniyyah*, p. 24. Besides, al-Mawardi maintains that if there is only one person who fulfills the requirements of imamate, it becomes his individual duty (*fard 'ayn*) to occupy the position, see *al-Ahkam as-Sultaniyyah*, p. 8.

[69]See for example: at-Tabari, *Tarikh*; also: Hasan and 'Ali Ibrahim, *an-Nuzum al-Islamiyyah*.

[70]Al-Mawardi, *al-Ahkam as-Sultaniyyah*, p. 7.

[71]*Ibid.*, p. 7

points out at another place that the bai'ah of 'Umar was settled by Abu Bakr irrespective of its subsequent approval or disapproval by others.[72]

On the other hand, al-Mawardi also mentions that the function of the ahl al-ikhtiyar is "to identify the man who will be appointed" as the imam.[73] This statement should not be taken out of context to support the argument that al-Mawardi saw the bai'ah of ahl al-ikhtiyar merely as a nomination of the most capable man for imamate while the appointment itself required a public decision. As has been shown earlier, al-Mawardi believes that the people have to follow the bai'ah of the ahl al-ikhtiyar as soon as it is offered by them.

Ibn Taimiyyah suggests that Abu Bakr's nomination of 'Umar as his successor became a legitimate bai'ah only after a majority of companions had agreed to it. He argues that imamate means a sovereignty and authority, which cannot be achieved by the approval of one or few persons unless such an approval also means the approval of enough people to allow him to effectively exercise his authority. However, Ibn Taimiyyah is of the view that the candidate for the imamate must have the bai'ah of those people who have effective power,[74] meaning that public support would come as a corollary of this initial bai'ah, not as a separate procedure required by itself. When Ibn Taimiyyah uses the term *jumhur sahaba* (a majority of the Prophet's companions), he is referring to leading companions among the immigrants from Makkah and their supporters in Medinah, not to every Bedouin who saw the Prophet and could technically be called a companion. This implicit public support is also mentioned by al-Ghazzali when he refers to "the one who is followed and obeyed [by others] and whose side the masses would take in important decisions."[75]

It is obvious, therefore, that the imam's legitimacy and effectiveness does not necessarily depend on instituting a separate arrangement for public approval. Such an assumption about the early caliphate, which is also held by some contemporary scho-

---

[72]*Ibid*, p. 10, but compare al-Juwayni, *Ghiyath al-Umam*, ed. F. 'Abd al-Mun'im, M. Hilmy (Alexandria: n.p., 1979), pp. 103-104.

[73]Al-Mawardi, *al-Ahkam as-Sultaniyyah*, p. 8.

[74]Ibn Taimiyyah, *Minhaj as-Sunnah an-Nabawiyyah*, vol. 1, p. 141.

[75]Al-Ghazzali, *Fada'ih al-Batiniyyah*, in Ibish, *Nusus*, pp. 313-314; *al-Iqtisad*, pp. 365-366.

lars,[76] cannot be supported by historical precedents or from juristic sources. However, we must keep in mind that all these precedents and opinions represent the exercise of ijtihad and are not necessarily binding for a contemporary Muslim state. Today, the parliamentary nomination of someone who is eligible and capable may serve the same purpose, or else a constitution may stipulate some other nominating method. Whatever methods are adopted in a given situation, they should not ignore the modern democratic experience in order to replicate the methods of bai'ah adopted in the early period of Islam. One must remember that the bai'ah of the early caliphs was itself an exercise of ijtihad, and each of the first four caliphs was chosen in a different way. The bai'ah represented a free expression of public choice, directly or through public representatives whose leadership was accepted by the people. It can be practiced through any suitable form.

The Imam's Nomination of His Successor: 'Istikhlaf al-'Ahd

The precedent of Abu Bakr's nomination of 'Umar as his successor was used by the jurists to justify the settlement of the bai'ah by one or a few persons of the ahl al-ikhtiyar, and to justify the nomination of a successor by the ruling imam. When juristic works began to be written, hereditary dynasties were already ruling most Muslim lands. Defending the principle of public choice as an alternative to the shi'i belief of a divine nomination of the imams, the sunni theologians and jurists faced a dilemma: the theory of public choice was no longer applied, and hereditary dynasties had become the rule of the day. They were inclined more to work out a justification, probably on the grounds that the form of the government was a matter of ijtihad, and the hereditary dynasties had already been accepted by the Muslims including prominent 'ulema as being in interest of the ummah. Implementing the theory of public choice in its true sense could therefore lead to continuous civil wars, rebellions, and bloodshed among people. The jurists also realized that it had become almost impossible for anyone to challenge military rulers who were supported by massive armies. It is in this context that the shift from ah al-hall wa al-'aqd to ah al-shawkah, as used by al-Ghazzali and Ibn Taimiyyah,[77] becomes understandable. Al-Mawardi as-

---

[76]See, for example, ar-Rayyis, *an-Nazariyyat as-Siyasiyah*, pp. 185-186.

[77]See, for example, al-Ghazzali, *Fada'ih al-Batiniyyah* and *al-Iqtisad* in Ibish, *Nusus*, pp. 313-314 and 365-366, respectively; Ibn Taimiyyah, *Minhaj as-Sunnah an-Nabawayyih*, vol. 1, p. 141.

sumes that the principle of an imam nominating his successor
had already been accepted by a consensus,[78] while al-Ghazzali
believes that an imam supported by ahl al-shawkah should be
accepted in the interest of enforcing the shari'ah and maintaining
the internal and external security of the Muslim lands. The fact
that these *de facto* rulers lacked some legally required qualifications was outweighed by the practical needs of the community.

However, jurists did try to provide some safeguards in case of
al-'ahd or al-istikhlaf in order to bring it closer to the original principle of public choice.

First, the jurists insisted that the successor must fulfill all the
requirements for the imamate at the time of his nomination and
actual succession.[80] As is well known, even this rule was ignored
by the monarchs. The jurists, however, only legitimized the imamate of those who fulfilled its requirements but were less
meritorious than some other available candidates (*imamat al-maf-
dul*).[81] Abu al-Hasan al-'Asha'ri, a prominent theologian, holds
that the bai'ah for one who is less meritorious would qualify him
as a king but not as an imam.[82] Al-Ghazzali is more flexible and
realistic; he thinks that the imam could always rely on others in
case he was not qualified to personally handle military and juristic matters. Moreover, the imam in such times, according to the
opinion of al-Ghazzali, does not have to be related to the tribe of
Quraysh.[83] He, along with other sunni theologians and jurists, believes that the less meritorious might be chosen as imam provided
he enjoyed asabiyyah. This, in their opinion, would secure unity
and order which are more important than outstanding moral behavior or juristic knowledge.[84]

The acceptance of the nominated successor was, according to

---

[78]Al-Mawardi, *al-Ahkam as-Sultaniyyah*, p. 10.

[79]Al-Ghazzali, *al-Iqtisad* in Ibish, *Nusus*, pp. 366-367.

[80]See, for example, al-Ash'ari, al-Baghdadi, Abu Ya'la, and al-Ghazali in the
selections of Ibish, *Nusus*, pp. 132-133, 136, 225-226, 316 seq.; 365-366; al-Mawardi,
al-Ahkam as-Sultaniyyah, p. 11; Abu Ya'la, *al-Ahkam as-Sultaniyyah*, p. 25.

[81]See, for example, al-Baqillani, al-Baghdadi, Abu Ya'la, al-Juwayni, and al-
Ghazali in the selections of Ibish, *Nusus*, pp. 54-55, 141, 218-219, 281-282, 330-331;
al-Mawardi, *al-Ahkam as-Sultaniyyah*, p. 8; Abu Ya'la, *al-Ahkam as-Sultaniyyah*,
p. 20.

[82]Reported by al-Baghdadi in his work, *Usul ud-Din*; see Ibish, *Nusus*, p. 141.

[83]Al-Ghazali, *Fada 'ih al-Batiniyyah* and *al-Iqtisad* in Ibish, *Nusus*, pp. 321, 329,
331, 365-367.

[84]Ibn Khaldun, *al-Muqaddimah*, pp. 193-196, 210 seq.

different juristic views, supposed to take place either after the nomination and before the succession, or at the actual time of succession. The jurists considered the imamate as a contract which required the free consent of both parties.[85] If the nominee was a minor and by the time he succeeded he had become an adult, what should be done? Al-Mawardi does not consider the nomination sufficient in such a case and requires the bai'ah of "ahl al-hall wa al-'aqd," apparently to make sure that the nominee fulfilled the requirements for the position at the time of his actual succession.[86]

Second, another safeguard in the case of 'ahd or istikhlaf was the approval of "ahl al-hall wa al-'aqd." Abu Ya'la made a clear distinction between the acts of nomination and the settlement of contract for the imamate. The right to nominate could be exercised by the existing imam but the bai'ah should be settled by "ahl al-hall wa al-'aqd" at the time of succession. As an extra precaution, the imam could not nominate the ahl al-ikhtiyar who would settle the bai'ah for his nominee.[87] Abu Ya'la's conception of al-'ahd or al-istikhlaf upholds the essential role of the public will in the choice of an imam, and has therefore been supported by the 'ulema.[88] Al-Mawardi's position, on the other hand, is that succession can be settled by the ruling imam himself without any recourse to the ahl al-ikhtiyar, provided the nominee is neither his father nor his son. In these two cases, al-Mawardi mentions three juristic views without pointing out his preference: one requires the consultation of ahl al-ikhtiyar, the nomination of father or son notwithstanding; another restricts this to the case where the nominee is the imam's son; and the third does not require any consultation in either of the two cases.[89]

Third, although kingship dominated Muslim lands, it was repeatedly emphasized by the jurists that the imamate was by no means a hereditary institution. This was clearly stated by al-

---

[85]Al-Mawardi, *al-Ahkam as-Sultaniyyah*, p. 11; see also p. 7; compare with Abu Ya'la, *al-Ahkam as-Sultaniyyah*, pp. 24-25.

[86]Al-Mawardi, *al-Ahkam as-Sultaniyyah*, p. 10.

[87]Abu Ya'la, *al Mu'tamad* in Ibish, *Nusus*, pp. 225-226; and *al-Ahkam as-Sultaniyyah*, pp. 25-26.

[88]See, for example, 'Abd al-Wahhab Khallaf, *as-Siyasah ash-Shar'iyyah* (Cairo: n.p., 1977), p. 58.

[89]Al-Mawardi, *al-Ahkam as-Sultaniyyah*, p. 10.

Baghdadi, Abu Ya'la,[90] Ibn Hazm,[91] and many others.[92] Al-Ju-wayni, for example, points out that the caliphate had acquired force and arrogance as its characteristic since the demise of the first four caliphs, and had turned into monarchy.[93] Even Ibn Khaldun, who elaborates at length upon asabiyyah and defends the nomination in general, and of Mu'awiyah's son Yazid in particular,[94] indicates clearly that the nomination for succession should not seek the creation of a family dynasty since this cannot be justified on religious grounds.[95]

Rule by Military Force: al-Ghalabah

The public contract of imamate, as a concept, was undermined not only by the Umayyads and others but also by military leaders who established themselves as overlords. Since the 2nd century A.H. / 8th C.E., several regions of the Islamic state fell under the rule of military leaders, and in the 3rd century A.H. / 9th C.E., the caliphate center itself came under the control of the Turkish military.[96]

As for the regional governorship, al-Mawardi and Abu Ya'la accept *de facto* situation as long as it is authorized by the caliph. A regional ruler could exercise complete authority in his realm subject to the condition that he recognize the ultimate authority of the caliph in matters pertaining to Islamic law. Al-Mawardi also believes that the imam and the regional ruler could share authority in certain areas such as the protection of the imamate, the unity of Muslim power against enemies, and the enforcement of

---

[90]Al-Baghdadi, *Usul ad-Din; Abu Ya'la, al-Mu'tamad* in Ibish, *Nusus*, pp. 135, 226-227.

[91]Ibn Hazm, *al-Fisal fi al-Milal wa an-Nihal*, vol. 4, p. 167.

[92]The Mu'tazilites seemed clear and firm in denouncing the inheritance of the imamate when they talked about 'Umayyads. However, they occasionally supported the rebellions of some of the descendants of the Prophet's family (*ahl al-Bayt*) who believed in the inheritance of the imamate. They also supported certain 'Abbassid caliphs who believed in the same doctrine. See, for example, *Rasa'il al-Jahiz*, vol. 2, ed. A. Harun (Cairo: n.p., 1965), pp. 7-16; ibn-Abi al-Hadid, *Sharh Nahj al-Balaghah*, vol. 2, ed. Abu al-Fadl Ibrahim (Cairo: n.p., 1959), p. 309; *al-Khayyat, al Intisar*, ed. D. Niberg (Cairo: n.p., 1925), p. 98; 'Abd al-Jabbar, *al-Mughni*, vol. 20 (Cairo: n.p., n.d.), p. 146; and al-Juwayni, *Ghiyath al-Umam*, p. 103.

[93]Al-Juwayni, *Ghiyath al-Umam*, p. 103.

[94]Ibn Khaldun *al-Muqaddimah*, pp. 202-298, 210-212.

[95]*Ibid*, p. 211.

[96]See, for a general survey, al Khudari, *ad-Dawla al-'Abbasiyyah*; Hasan Ibrahim, *Tarikh al-Islam*, vols. 3, 4.

Islamic civil and penal laws.[97] Al-Mawardi further believes that a regional ruler, to be legitimate, must be a pious Muslim. In principle, both al-Mawardi and Abu Ya'la consider a regional governor as a public representative who would keep his position even after the imam's death. The minister, on the other hand, was a representative of the imam and thus would lose his position automatically upon the imam's death.[98]

At the level of imamate, al-Mawardi would accept any *de facto* authority if it did not disobey the imam. All decisions of such an interdictor on the imam's authority could be approved by the latter as long as they followed the rules of faith and justice so that public affairs might not deteriorate. If these decisions violated those rules, the imam could reject them and ask some other power to remove that interdictory authority.[99] Abu Ya'la agrees with al-Mawardi on this question and believes that the imam would have no option but to seek the removal of the authority in question by force.[100]

Al-Ghazzali accepts the reality of the Turkish power which had become dominant in his time and legitimized it on the grounds that it was supportive of the caliphate.[101] He also shows considerable flexibility in determining the requirements for the imamate and strongly defends the legitimacy of the imamate of the 'Abbassid caliph al-Mustazhir bi-Allah[102] (487 512 A.H. / 1094-1119 C.E.), who ruled at a time when Turkish power was predominant. He believes that the enforcement of Islamic law, the fulfillment of public needs, and the maintenance of peace were more important than the strict fulfillment of certain juristic requirements. Some other theologians, including al-Juwayni[103] and al-Taftanzani,[104] also accept the status quo of Turkish power on similar grounds. Ibn Khaldun believes that in the absence of an asabiyyah which could unite the Muslims under one Islamic state, establishing regional power centers would be advisable.[105] The

---

[97]Al-Mawardi, *al-Ahkam as-Sultaniyyah*, pp. 33-34; Abu Ya'la, *al-Ahkam as-Sultaniyyah*, pp. 37-38.

[98]*Ibid*, pp. 32, 36.

[99]Al-Mawardi, *al-Ahkam as-Sultaniyyah*, pp. 19-20.

[100]Abu Ya'la, *al-Ahkam as-Sultaniyyah*, pp. 22-24.

[101]Al-Ghazali, *Fada'ih al-Batiniyyah*, in Ibish, *Nusus*, pp. 319-321.

[102]*Ibid*, pp. 306-316; also, *al-Iqtisad ibid*, p. 366.

[103]Al-Juwayni, *Ghiyath al-Umam*, pp. 247-250.

[104]Al-Taftanzani, *Sharh al-'Aqa'id an-Nasafiyyah*(Cairo: n.p., 1913), pp. 483-484.

[105]Ibn Khaldun, *al-Muqaddimah*, p. 196.

Hanafi jurist Badr al-Din ibn Jama'a (d. 734 A.H. / 1333 C.E.) recommends that the most powerful among those who enjoyed
shawkah should be obeyed to keep public order and unity even
if he was ignorant or deviated from acceptable behavior. He
suggests that anyone who was strong enough to depose the existing ruler should be obeyed by the people. It is obvious that
Jama'a was simply presenting a juristic formulation of what already existed in Egypt under the Mamelukes.[106]

The Dissolution of the Bai'ah Contract: Removal of the Imam

The right of dissolving a contract cannot legally be separated
from the right of undertaking it. Nevertheless, the bitter experience of the rebellion against, and assassination of 'Uthman led to
disputes about succession and legitimate political authority which
eventually discouraged others from exercising this right. Theologians and jurists were therefore reluctant to support the dissolution of a bai'ah contract and the removal of an imam. The
Ash'arite theologian al-Baqillani rejects such a dissolution in principle, especially when, even though he fulfilled all the requirements of his position, the people wanted a new imam for the sake
of change only. This does not mean that a time limit for an
imam's rule is not legitimate. Both historical practice and juristic
formulations indicate that the imam would continue to hold his
position as long as he fulfilled his responsibilities. In our view, it
is a discretionary matter which has been left to (qualified) people
to decide through ijtihad. If a certain period is specified, the contract would only be terminated at the end of the stipulated period,
not dissolved. However, Al-Baqillani mentions elsewhere that an
imam should be deposed if he becomes an apostate, neglects the
performance of prayers and invites others to do the same, or else
becomes physically handicapped. Persistent debauchery and immoral behavior (fisq), injustice (jawr) in public behavior, and neg-
ligence of the Islamic laws also justify the removal of an imam.
However, most jurists and traditionists (ahl al-hadith) believed, as
al-Baqillani indicated, that in such a case the imam should only
be advised and admonished or, at the most, might be disobeyed
when his orders clearly violate the teachings of Islam. According
to this opinion, debauchery could be a sufficient reason to refuse
the bai'ah at the time of his nomination, but would not be enough
to depose him after the bai'ah has been concluded.[107] Al-Nasafi,

---

[106]Ibn Jama'a, *Tahrir al-Ahakam fi-Tadbir Adl al-Islam Islamica*, No. Vi, 1934; see
also H.A.R. Gibb, *Studies in the Civilization of Islam.*

[107]Al-Baqillani, *at-Tamhid* in Ibish, *Nusus*, pp. 50, 57-58.

al-Taftanzani and an-Nawawi also hold this view.[108] Al-Mawardi differentiates between cases of losing legal acceptability (*'adalah*) or physical fitness which could deprive an imam of his ability to fulfill his obligations, and cases which would not hurt his ability to function. One can clearly see that al-Mawardi is trying to minimize the number of cases which might justify the imam's removal. This is significant because he was a follower of ash-Shaf'i who favored removing an imam if the latter was found guilty of debauchery and injustice.[109] The Shaf'iyyah also hold that the imam might be tried for his debauchery and other crimes.[110] Al-Mawardi reports that one jurist in Basra believed that a deviation from Islamic norms would not automatically lead to an imam's dismissal if he could substantiate his actions with a rationale. The only acceptable reason in al-Mawardi's view for removing an imam was the permanent loss of mental or physical fitness, such as insanity, blindness, and amputation of both hands or legs, or if he was captured by an enemy and could not obtain his freedom.[111]

Abu Ya'la also believes that the imamate contract could not be dissolved as long as there were no valid reasons for doing so. An imam should resign when he feels he has developed some permanent deficiency, but as long as he is fit to perform his duties as an imam, he cannot resign his position.[112]

Al-Juwayni holds that if an imam is immoral and deviates from the required behavior, he may step down, but for others to depose him, ijtihad would be necessary in each case. Ironically, he also holds that an imam can resign his position anytime he likes.[113] Other theologians and jurists including al-Baghdadi, al-Ijy, al-Jurjani and Ibn Hazm support the imam's removal if the

[108]Al-Taftanzani, *Sharh al-'Aqa'id al-Nasafiyyah*, p. 488; al-Nawawi, *Sharh Sahih Muslim*, vol. 2 (Cairo), p. 229.

[109]Al-Taftanzani, *Sharh al-'Aqa'id al-Nasafiyyah*, p. 488.

[110]Shaf'i jurists stated that if the *imam* committed adultery, he need not be deposed, but the legal penalty (*al-hadd*) would be administered by one of his deputies. The Hanafiyyah stated that the *imam* should only be punished in cases of *qisas* (for any corporal assault) or deferment of financial obligations, but not in cases of *hudud* (for crimes of adultery, calumniation, armed assaults [*hirabah*], ...); see M. Shaltut, *Fiqh al-Qur'an wa as-Sunna* (Cairo: n.p., n.d.), pp. 96-97.

[111]Al-Mawardi, *al-Ahkam as-Sultaniyyah*, pp. 17-20.

[112]Abu Ya'la, *al-Mu'tamad* in Ibish, *Nusus*, pp. 213-214, 216-218; *al-Ahkam as-Sultaniyyah*, pp. 20-23, 28.

[113]Al-Juwayni, *al-Irshah* in Ibish, *Nusus*, p. 279.

situation of the people or the condition of the faith was deteriorating, or if the imam was habitually[114] unjust. The Mu'tazilites also believed that an imam should be replaced if he committed fisq, even if it did not reach the level of apostasy and injustice.[115]

The Principle of Shura

Public participation in reaching important political decisions is a basic principle of Muslim society and state. It was this principle which was applied in the contract of imamate or bai'ah in the past, and it could very well be applied in any public voting today. The Prophet himself was ordered by God to conduct shura with his companions in any worldly matter where there was no revelation: "Forgive them [the companions] and pray for them, and take counsel with them in all matters of public concern, then when you have decided [upon a course of action], place your trust in Allah" (āl-'Imrān 3:159). Shura (counsel) is mentioned in the Qur'an as a main Islamic trait which is integrally related to obedience to God, the performance of prayers, and spending out of what one is granted by God for social needs. The Qur'an says: "...and those who respond to the call of their Sustainer and are constant in prayer, and whose rule [in all matters of common concern] is consultation among themselves and who spend out of what we provide for them..." (ash-Shura: 38). The principle of shura is to be applied at all levels of social interactions. The family, the smallest unit of social structure, is also asked to practice shura before deciding upon important issues. The Qur'an taught parents to discuss a child's weaning through an exchange of views (shura): "...and if both parents decide by mutual consent and counsel upon weaning the child, they are permitted to do..." (al-Baqara: 233). According to many commentators, shura was obligatory even for the Prophet himself. Some commentators hold that it was only a recommendation for the Prophet because of his special status as a messenger of God.[116] He, however, practiced shura and followed the advice of his companions on several occasions, for example, during his campaigns of Badr, Uhud, al-Khandaq, and Hudaibiyyah. Even in a sensitive situation, such as allegations against his wife 'Aishah, the Prophet discussed it

---

[114]Al-Baghdadi, Usul ad-Din (Istanbul: 1928), p. 278; al-Jurjan, Sharh al-Mawaqif (of al-Ijy, vol. 3 (Cairo: n.p., 1311 A.H.), p. 267; Ibn Hazm, al-Fisal, vol. 4 (Cairo: n.p., 1321 A.H.), p. 102.

[115]'Abd al-Jabbar, al-Mughni, vol. 15 (Cairo: n.p., n.d.), p. 251; vol. 20, part 1, pp. 53, 96, 310, part 2, pp. 170 seq.; ibn Abi al-Hadid, Sharh Nahj al-Balaghah, vol. 9, p. 294.

[116]Ibn Kathir, Tafsir, vol. 1, commentary on: 3/159; al-Fakhr ar-Razi, Tafsir, vol. 3, commentary on the same verse.

in public and asked for advice.[117]

It has been argued that although shura is an Islamic duty to be observed by the imam, he is not obligated to follow the resulting advice. This view, which considers shura as consultative and optional, negates its very spirit. Ibn Kathir reports on the authority of 'Ali ibn Abi Talib that the Prophet was asked about 'the decision' (al-azn) mentioned in the Qur'anic verse, "...and take counsel with them in all matters of public concern, then when you have decided upon a course of action place your trust in God..." (āl-'Imrān: 159). The Prophet, upon whom be peace, replied that it means "taking the counsel of those who are known for their good opinions and then following it."[118] Al-Hasan ibn 'Ali is reported to have said that the Prophet was in no need of shura because he was guided by the divine revelation, but that God had ordered him to practice shura as an example for the Muslims. It was reported by Abu Hurairah that the Prophet practiced shura with his companions more frequently than anyone else he had ever seen.[119] The first caliph, Abu Bakr, held a shura before sending the expedition against those who refused to pay zakah. He did this after he was able to convince those who differed with him to support his action. The second caliph followed shura in many military and administrative affairs, such as his campaigns against the Sassanid Empire and Egypt, the establishment of the revenue department (dīwan), and the imposition of kharaj. In this, he did not make any distinction between Muslims and non-Muslims.[120] Ibn 'Atiyyah, a famous commentator of the Qur'an, emphatically declares that "shura is basic to the shari'ah and represents one of its obligatory rules. Any [ruler] who does not seek the counsel of learned and religious people should be replaced."[121] According to al-Bukhari, the imams who came after

---

[117]Ibn Kathir, Tafsir, vol. 1, commentary on 3/159; see also al-Bidaiya wa an-Nihaya, vols. 3-5; Ibn Hisham, Sirat an-Nabi.

[118]Ibn Kathir, Tafsir, vol. 1, commentary on 3/159.

[119]Az-Zamakhshari, al-Kashshaf, vol. 1, commentary on 3/159; al-Qurtubi, Tafsir, vol. 4, commentary on the same verse; vol. 16, commentary on: 42/38; al-Tabari, Tafsir, vol. 4, commentary on: 3/159; Ibn Taimiyyah, as-Siyasah ash-Shar'iyyah, p. 158.

[120]Al-Qurtubi, Tafsir, vol. 16, commentary on 42/38; also Abu Yusuf, al-Kharaj, 4th ed. (Cairo: n.p., 1392 A.H.), pp. 40-41; Ibn Abd al-Hakam, Futuh Misr wa al-Maghreb ed. A. Amer (Cairo: n.p., 1961), p. 216; al-Baladhuri, Futuh al-Buldan, ed. R.M. Radwan, Beirut 1978, pp. 216-217, 300, 435-436, 444; al-Mawardi, al-Ahkam as-Sultaniyyah, pp. 199-200.

[121]Al-Qurtubi, Tafsir, vol. 4, p. 249; Abu Hayyan, al-Bahr al-Muhit, vol. 3, p. 99; ash-Shawkani, Fath al-Qadir, vol. 1, p. 360.

the early caliphs practiced shura extensively on all matters for which no clear injunctions were to be found in the Qur'an and Sunnah.[122] Ibn Taimiyyah holds that shura is indispensable for Muslim authorities (ulu'l-'amr), and that even if the Prophet resorted to it in matters where no revelation was available, this is all the more obligatory for others to do so.[123]

Some jurists have argued that ijma' (consensus) is also integrally related to the principle of shura. The Qur'anic verse "Obey God, and obey the Messenger and those among you who have been entrusted with authority" (an-Nisa': 59) has been interpreted by Muhammad Rashid Rida as referring to the ijma' of the Muslim people, and not that of the 'ulema or *mujtahid*.[124] Most commentators on the Qur'an as well as jurists take the term "ulu'l-'amr" to mean both the rulers and 'ulema together,[125] while some of them say that it refers only to the "ahl al-hall wa al-'aqd."[126] Al-Qurtubi reports an interesting interpretation by Ibn Kaysan which does not restrict the concept of ulu'l-'amr to the 'ulema only, but also includes those who are intelligent, wise, and engaged in the management of public affairs.[127] According to this interpretation, obedience to the "ahl al-hall wa al-'aqd" or ahl al-shura would be obligatory on both the ruler as well as the people. Al-Qurtubi reports on the authority of Ibn Khuwayz Mindad that rulers should consult the 'ulema on religious and juristic problems, military experts on military affairs, distinguished public figures on welfare, and ministers, secretaries and local governors on the country's development. The idea was to have consultants who were experts in various functional areas of religious and worldly concerns.[127] According to to Rashid Rida, their decision would represent the ijma' which, according to traditions, is divinely guided. The imam, therefore, is obligated to carry out their decision. If he rejects it, he would not only be violating one of the basic principles of an Islamic state (at-Tur:38) but would also be negating the ob-

---

[122]Al-Qurtubi, *Tafsir*, vol. 4, p. 251.

[123]Ibn Taimiyyah, *as-Siyasah ash-Shar'iyyah*, pp. 157-158.

[124]*Tafsir al-Manar*, vol. 5, pp. 201-214.

[125]See, for example, the commentaries on 3/59 of Ibn Kathir, vol. 1, al-Qurtubi, vol. 5, pp. 259-260; and Ibn Taimiyyah, *as-Siyasah ash-Shar'iyyah*, p. 159.

[126]See the commentary on the same verse by al-Fakhr ar-Razi; also see *Tafsir al-Manar*, vol. 5, pp. 182-185.

[127]Al-Qurtubi, *Tafsir*, vol. 5, p. 260.

[128]*Ibid*, pp. 250-51.

ligatory authority of ijma' (āl-'Imrān: 59).[129]

It has been pointed out that complete reliance on majority decision is not supported by Islam. It is true that there are several Qur'anic verses which say that the majority does not necessarily follow the right path.[130] Still, the argument here is not about the human need for divine guidance in matters of faith, ethics, and laws of rights and wrongs. No majority can change these permanent norms and precepts as enunciated in the Qur'an and Sunnah. It is only in worldly matters and transitory affairs about which no relevant text in the Qur'an and Sunnah is found that decisions of shura would be binding. As a contemporary jurist points out, while following the majority opinion may be wrong in matters of belief and faith, it would be equally wrong to disregard the majority views on how to manage material affairs and public benefits.[131] Another jurist holds that the disparagement of the majority in the Qur'an refers only to disbelievers not to Muslims who are guided individually and collectively by the teachings of the Qur'an and Sunnah.[132]

We find numerous references to the majority principle in both historical precedents and juristic writings. Ibn Taimiyyah, for example, emphasizes that 'Umar became caliph by the bai'ah of the majority of the companions, and not merely by the nomination of his predecessor Abu Bakr. Similarly, when 'Umar nominated a committee of six to choose his successor, he said that the committee should decide by a majority vote, and if they were equally divided, 'Abd Allah ibn 'Umar would have the casting vote. Historian Sheikh M. al-Khudari agrees with this formulation and regrets that the institution of shura, as known to the early

---

[129]See, for example, R. az-Zalabani, *as-Siyasah ad-Dasturiyyah Ash-Shari'yyah*, in *al-Azhar*, vol. 18, no. 2.

[130]See, for example, the following Qur'anic verses: "But most people do not know (this fact)." (12:21, 40); "Yet however strongly you may desire it, most people will not believe (in this revelation). (12:103); "Now if you obey the majority of those who live on the earth, they will lead you astray from the path of God; they follow but conjectures and they only guess." (6:116); "There is no comparison between the bad things and the good things even if you are pleased by the plenty of bad things." (5:100).

[131]M.A. al-'Arabi, *at-Tanzim al-Hadith lid-Dawla al-Islamiyyah bayna ash-Shari'ah wa al-Qanun*, quoted in A.I. al-Ansari, *ash-Shurah* (Cairo: n.p., 1981), pp. 183-185.

[132]A. 'Abd al-Khaliq, *ash-Shurah fi zill an-Nizam al-Islami* (Kuwait: n.p., 1975), pp. 105-106.

Muslims, did not develop in later eras.[133] The jurists also agree
that the selection of imams for the local mosque should be done
by the majority of the people concerned and not by the government.[134] Al-Ghazzali, while discussing the case of bai'ah for two
imams, states that preference is to be given to the one with the
most supporters. The traditions of the Prophet also emphasize the
importance of the majority. Thus, the sunnis called themselves the
"people of sunnah and jama'a" (*ahl al-sunnah wa al-jama'a*). The
jurists established as one of their fundamentals (*usul*) that the
majority could provide sufficient support (*hujja*) for a view even
if it did not enjoy the obligation of an ijma'. They also maintained
that, as a general rule, a majority should constitute the basis for
a juristic decision when no other evidence was available.[135]

A lucid elaboration of the principle of shura and the role of the
majority opinion in Islam is found in Muhammad Asad's *The Principles of State and Government in Islam*. Asad explains:

> In an Islamic state, a continuous temporal legislation
> would relate to many problems of administration not
> touched upon by the shari'ah as well as the problems
> with regard to which the shari'ah has provided general
> principles but no detailed laws. In either instance, it is up
> to the community to evolve the relevant detailed legisla-
> tion through an exercise of independent reasoning (ijtihad)
> in consonance with the spirit of Islamic law and the best
> interests of the people. It goes without saying that in mat-
> ters affecting the communal side of our life, no ijtihadi de-
> cisions can be left to the discretion of individuals; they
> must be based on a definite consensus (ijma') of the whole
> community (which of course does not preclude the com-
> munity's agreement in any matter under consideration on
> an ijtihadi finding arrived at previously by an individual
> scholar or a group of scholars). Who is to enact this tem-
> poral communal legislation? ... An individual, however
> brilliant, righteous, and well-intentioned, may easily com-
> mit mistakes ... (Besides), possession of absolute power
> often corrupts its possessor and tempts him to abuse it
> consciously or unconsciously ... The legislative powers of
> the state should be vested in a body of legislators whom

---

[133]M. al-Khudari, "Nuzum al-Hukm fi 'Ahd ar-Rashidin" (chapter's title), *Muhadarat
Tarikh al-Umam al-Islamiyyah*; see also the commentary of A. 'Abd al-Khaliq on
the same event, *ash-Shurah*, p. 104.

[134]Al-Mawardi, *al-Ahkam as-Sultaniyyah*, p. 102.

[135]Al-Rayyis, *an-Nazariyyat as-Siyasiyyah*, pp. 250 seq; see the quotations of ar-
Rayyis with others in al-Ansari, *ash-Shurah*, pp. 178-179.

the community would elect for this specific purpose ... The Qur'anic injunction about shura (42:38) must be regarded as the fundamental operative clause of all Islamic thought relating to statecraft ... The phrase (*amruhum shura baynahum*) — literally: their communal business is consultation among themselves — makes the transaction of all political business not only consequent to but synonymous with consultation, which means that the legislative powers of the state must be vested in an assembly chosen by the community specifically for this purpose ... In view of the obvious shortcomings of most of the so-called democratic systems prevailing in the modern West, some contemporary Muslims dislike the idea of making the legislature in an Islamic state dependent on a mere counting of votes. The bare fact, so they argue, that a legislative measure has been supported by a majority does not necessarily imply that it is a right measure ... The objective truth of this view cannot be disputed. The human mind is extremely fallible; moreover, men do not always follow the promptings of right and equity, and the history of the world is full of instances of wrong decisions made by a foolish or selfish majority in spite of the warnings of a wiser minority. Nevertheless, it is difficult to see what alternative could be within a legislative body to the principle of majority decisions. Who is to establish from case to case whether the majority or the minority is right? ... One might of course suggest that the final verdict should rest with the *emir* (or imam) ... but is it not equally possible that he is mistaken while the view of the majority is right? The critics usually answer that the amir must be chosen on the grounds of his superior wisdom and righteousness ... Is it not equally true that the Muslims are supposed to elect the *majlis* (assembly) on the basis of the wisdom and righteousness attributable to each candidate? ... A perfect guarantee is unfortunately beyond human reach. The best we can hope for is that when an assembly composed of reasonable persons discusses a problem, the majority of them will finally agree upon a decision which in all probability will be right. It is for this reason that the Prophet strongly and on many occasions admonished the Muslims "Follow the largest group ... (reported by Ibn Majah on the authority of 'Abd Allah ibn Umar), "It is your duty to stand by the united community and the majority ..." (reported by Ibn Hanbal on the authority of Mu'adh ibn Jabal). In fact, human ingenuity has not evolved a better method for corporate decisions than the majority principle. No doubt a majority can err, but so can a minority ... The fallibility of the human mind makes the committing of errors an inescapable factor of human life, and so we have no choice but to learn through trial and error and subsequent correction."[136]

It is true that the 'ulema, as scholars and experts of shari'ah, constitute an integral part of the legislative process in an Islamic state. According to one interpretation of an-Nisa': 59, the 'ulema are the core participants in the legislative decisions of an Islamic state.[137] Yet, it would be incorrect to describe these arrangements as leading to some kind of theocracy. The 'ulema neither represent a closed class nor do they enjoy any theocratic privileges. They will be joined in the decision-making process by experts in economics, commerce, health, education, science, and technology who, besides their own specializations, will have sufficient knowledge of Islam, especially as it relates to their own areas of concerns.[138] This is in consonance with the principles of ijtihad as formulated by the jurists.[139]

Differences may arise between the imam and the shura. If such differences are discretionary and are related to issues of public interest, the majority view in the shura should prevail. If the differences are related to the interpretation of legal norms and the observance of the Qur'an and Sunnah, they should be discussed first in a joint session consisting of an equal number of the 'ulema in the assembly and juristic experts of the government. If such a meeting fails to reach a solution, the case may be referred to a constitutional court, the supreme court, or any other similar judicial body empowered to adjudicate. In the case of serious political accusations against an imam, the assembly and/or supreme judicial body may conduct the trial in accordance with special regulations devised for such situations. The assembly and the court may deal with the case either independently or in cooperation with each other. Some safety checks may be added for the

---

[136]Muhammad Asad, *The Principles of State and Government in Islam*, (Gibraltar: Dar al-Andalus, 1982), pp. 43-50.

[137]See, for example, al Qurtubi, *Tafsir*, the commentary on an-Nisa':59, especially vol. 5, pp. 259-260.

[138]See M. K. Wasfi, *Madkhal an-Nuzum al-Islamiyyah*, pp. 128-129. The author emphasizes that scholars who combine knowledge in a certain field with the knowledge of Islam would be accorded recognition in an Islamic state according to their knowledge of Islam, not in another specialty.

[139]'Abd-Allah at-Turki, *Usul Madhab Ahmad*, 2nd ed. (Riyadh: n.p., 1977), pp. 630-631, quoting Ibn Taimiyyah in his work, *al-Majmu'*, and Ibn al-Qayyim in his work, *I'lam al-Muwaqqi'in*.

removal of the imam in order to make sure that the system is not trivialized and misused for petty purposes. The procedure suggested here to deal with the cases of differences between the imam and shura follow the Qur'anic injunction contained in the last part of the verse 59 in an-Nisa' which says that: "... if you are at variance over any matter, refer it to Allah and His Messenger if you [truly] believe in Allah and the Last Day. This is the best [for you] and the most suitable for reaching the right decision."

The Super Rules Which Control the Islamic Authorities

In addition to theoretical limits which modern Western thinkers have attempted to place on the ruler's authority, attempts have also been made to identify certain super rules, which are supposedly inviolable even for a sovereign. The classical notion of natural law was one such attempt. One may argue, however, that this concept is as inadequate as that of the social contract to ensure meaningful checks on the ruler's authority.

According to Islam, "super rules" which control the behavior of individuals, society, and the state are in the Qur'an and the Sunnah of the Prophet. The rulers and jurists are free to find new solutions for emerging problems in their society, if no relevant text in the Qur'an or the Sunnah can be applied to the case. However, these new solutions reached by ijtihad or by any other practice must not violate the text of the Qur'an and Sunnah. The observance of the goals (*maqasid*) of the shari'ah and its general principles as enunciated in the revealed sources is fundamental for ijtihad.[140] How can a Muslim ruler, for example, ever ignore the guidance of these principles indicated in the following Qur'anic verse:

> Allah commands justice, the doing of good and generosity toward [one's] fellow men, and He forbids all indecency, bad deeds and aggression; He exhorts you [repeatedly] so that you might bear [all this] in mind.

> Those who shall follow the Messenger, the unlettered Prophet ... [who] will enjoin upon them the doing of what is right and forbid them the doing of what is wrong, and make lawful to them the good things of life and forbid them the bad things, and lift from them their burdens and the shackles that were upon them [aforetime]" (al-A'raf:157).

---

[140]Ash-Shatibi, *al-Muwafaqat*, vol. 4, pp. 105-107.

How can anyone ever neglect this precisely formulated principle which the Prophet expressed lucidly and sharply in these few words: "Nobody is allowed to harm anybody — whether deliberately (dirar) or not darar."

The Islamic state is very close to what is presently called an ideological state, although we cannot use this term because an ideology is based on human ideas, not divine revelation. Nevertheless, it is not a theocratic state ruled by a privileged oligarchy of clergy or by divinely inspired rulers who are empowered to define the perimeters of right and wrong. The Islamic state is bound by certain general and permanent super rules which are contained in the Qur'an and Sunnah. These rules direct and control all the decisions and actions of the state. They are also derived from revealed sources and are therefore more effectively employed than the rules formulated under such concepts as natural law, social solidarity, and human rights. In addition, they are different from the concept of public order, which cannot be surpassed by any private agreement as in some liberal states, because this concept is flexible and differs from one field of human activity to another. Public order is not permanent, uniform, or universal. Moreover, it is supposed to be equal with the law since it is often established by law, and hence, it is inferior to the constitution and cannot contest any of its rules. This is not true for super rules in general, and the Islamic super rules as presented in the Qur'an and Sunnah enjoy absolute superiority over man-made legislation. Accordingly, a superior legality is to be expected in the exercise of authority which is limited by the super rules on the one hand and by the demands of public satisfaction on the other.[141]

One of the paramount super rules in an Islamic state relates to the Qur'anic injunction to "enjoin right and forbid evil" (al-Hajj: 41). The Islamic state discharges its responsibility through a network of administrative and judicial institutions. However, as the jurists have pointed out, this does not give licence to the state to interfere in the private lives of individual citizens and to violate the sanctity of the rights given to them by God.[142]

---

[141]M.K. Wasfi, Madkhal an-Nuzum al-Islamiyyah, pp. 45-51, 87-101. For the general objectives (maqasid) of the shari'ah see: ash-Shatibi al-Muwafaqat, vol. 2, ed. A. Diraz (Cairo: n.p., n.d.), pp. 6 seq., specially pp. 6-25; Khallaf, 'Ilm Usul al-Fiqh, (Kuwait: n.p., 1978), pp. 197-210; also: At-Tahir 'Ashur, Maqasid al-Shari'ah, (Tunis: n.p., n.d.).

[142]Abu Ya'la, al-Ahkam as-Sultaniyyah, pp. 285-286, 295-297, 300.

Islamic law relies primarily on a spiritual and moral basis, but it does not ignore the importance of formulating rules which must guide and control individual and collective behavior. People have not been left to pick up "super rules" from their own subjective feelings; these have been clearly prescribed in the Qur'an and Sunnah. Islam does not leave any ambiguity about what is right and what is wrong, what is good and what is evil, and what is just and what is unjust.

"These are the limits ordained by God, so do not transgress them. If any do transgress the limits ordained by God, such persons are evildoers" (al-Baqarah: 229).

However, these super rules and divine principles cannot be effectively employed unless they rely on the faith and piety of the people. In Islam, law and conscience support each other in building the Muslim individual, society, and state: "The only response of believers, whenever they are summoned unto God and His Messenger in order that [the divine writ] may judge between them, can be no other than: 'We have heard, and we pay heed!' It is they, who will attain a happy state" (an-Nur: 51).

THE PRINCIPLE OF SHURA AND THE ROLE OF THE UMMAH IN ISLAM

Fazlur Rahman

Muslims — or at least the vast majority of them — have been very vocal about the need to establish an Islamic state somewhere in the world, or, if it is impossible to set up a unitary Islamic state, at least several Islamic states. The idea of an Islamic state has many implications touching both its form and substance and raises questions on the unity and multiplicity of such states, the nature of legislation and source of power, and whether or not it ought to be a democracy. In this paper, I shall discuss this last question, which concerns not only the form of the state but which has obvious far-reaching consequences for substantive issues as well — for example, the source of power and the nature of legislation.

Although Muslims have been involved in long and passionate discussions about the need for an Islamic state, there is as yet little consensus on any of the preceding basic matters, particularly its form. Yet, the importance of the issue cannot be denied since it is fundamentally related to the question of the Muslim *ummah* (people) and the nature of its role in an Islamic state. We will first try to delineate the bearing which the teachings of the Qur'an have on the subject, then briefly characterize both the views of classical Muslim jurists and the practice of the community in the past. Then, we will give the essentials of the current positions and, finally, indicate our conclusion.

The Qur'an formally announced the establishment of the Muslim community in Medinah in connection with three events: the declaration that all Muslims must undertake the *hajj* (pilgrimage) to Makkah, that *jihad* (struggle in the way of Allah) is obligatory, and that the qiblah's direction is changed from Jerusalem to the Ka'bah in Makkah. We will not go into the timing of these events for it has no direct bearing on our present problem. It is sufficient to point out that the pilgrimage was announced first, then probably came jihad, and then the change in the qiblah. Be that as it may, the hajj and jihad are treated in close proximity to each other in *surah* 22 (al-Hajj), while the hajj and the change of the qiblah appear close to each other in surah 2 (al-Baqarah), both surahs being contemporary or revealed within a short time span.

All three events are thus closely related.

It is also obvious that all three have a direct impact on the community's life and constitution. It is, therefore, hardly surprising that in both places the Qur'an talks about the ummah and its role. The community, according to the Qur'an, is a "median community" so that it can be a "witness upon mankind" — mediate their extreme positions and balance them out: "And even so have We appointed you as a median community, that you may be witness over men" (al-Baqarah 2:142). What the Qur'an probably has in mind is the balancing effect of the Muslim community on the immobility or rigidity of Jewish particularism on the one hand and the excessively "accommodating" nature of Christianity on the other. Of course, this immediate objective of the Qur'an can and must be extended by the principle of *qiyas* (analogy) to other extremes, for example, between communism and capitalism. The term "witness" here, as the Qur'anic commentators remind us, refers to the balance of the two sides of a scale. The idea, then, is that Muslims are the scale or the judge whereby extremes are to be determined, and they are also the modifiers whereby those extremes are to be smoothed out. The former is an intellectual or diagnostic role, while the latter is an operational one.

Al-Hajj: 40 states: "Those [are Muslims] who, when We give them power on the earth, shall establish prayers, pay *zakah*, command good and prohibit evil — and to God belongs the end of the affairs." Al-'Imrān: 110 says to the same effect: "You are the best community produced for mankind, for you command good and prohibit evil, and you believe in God." The community's task, then, is to establish order on the earth by prohibiting evil and commanding good on the basis of belief in a unique God. That this order will be a sociopolitical one erected on a valid and viable ethical basis is, I think, obvious from the wording of both these passages of the Qur'an. In fact, establishing such an order and "witness" over mankind are fundamentally interdependent; neither is possible without the other.

The preceding verses talk about the role of the Muslim community in the world at large; they do not talk about its internal constitution or structure. However, āl-Imrān: 103 has often been interpreted as referring to this internal structure. It reads: "Let there be of you a community who calls [people] to virtue, commands good and prohibits evil — these shall be the successful ones." Here the words "let there be of you a community" can be read, in the original Arabic, in two ways: "Let you be a community" or "Let there be *from among* you a community or a group." Taking the words in the latter sense, it has often been claimed that this verse refers to the learned Muslims, meaning the religious leadership whose task it is to call people (Muslims) to righteousness, command good, and prohibit evil. It is difficult to see how the Qur'an could confer this duty upon the religious leadership, for in the other verses discussed earlier, this phrase refers to a general socio-political function, which makes it unlikely that here it refers to religious leadership. It is more probable that this verse, like the other two, also refers to the role of the Muslim community in general, namely, establishing an ethically based sociopolitical order.

There is no doubt that the Qur'an calls upon Muslim people with an insightful understanding of the faith. "Why should there not turn up from every division [of Muslims] a group in order that they might understand the faith deeper and, when they return to their people, they might admonish them so that their brethren can also improve their conduct by desisting [from possible mistakes]."[1] It is obvious from this verse that the religious leadership has to acquire a deep understanding of the faith and then teach it to others. If this function can be refered to as "comanding good and prohibiting evil" in some sence, then the religious scholars can be called "people who command good and prohibit evil." This, however, detracts from the meaningful sense in which the community as a whole has been given that title or the sense in which the duly constituted political or administrative authority in Islam has been called "ulu'l-amr" by the Qur'an.[2]

Indeed, the task devolving upon the religious leadership is twofold: the acquisition of correct and meaningful knowledge of the faith and its diffusion through teaching and preaching. They do not constitute an elite above any other functional group for the Qur'an abhors the idea of elitism so much that it unequivocally states that all Muslims are responsibe for "prohibiting evil and commanding good," and "Believing men and believing women are friends and supporters of each other: they command good and prohibit evil, establish prayers, pay zakah, and obey God and His Messenger — these are the ones upon whom God is going to have His mercy; God is mighty and wise."[3]

Since this verse speaks about the mutual support and friendship of Muslims, it can be seen as regulating the internal relationship of the community, but here "commanding good and prohibiting

---

[1] The Qur'an 9:122
[2] The Qur'an 4:59, 83
[3] The Qur'an 9:122

evil" is stated to be the duty and privilege of every Muslim. There is not the slightest suggestion of an elite that can arrogate to itself this particular function in the name of superior knowledge, understanding, or wisdom. This is both a restatement and corroboration of what the Qur'an often states to be the sole basis of mutual relationships among Muslims – that is, active good will for and cooperation with each other: "Those who believe and mutually admonish each other with steadfastness and mutual mercy."[4] Again, "Those who believe, do good works and support each other by admonishing with the truth and with steadfastness."[5] On cooperation, we have in al-An'ām: 2, "... cooperate on the basis of goodness and warning each other against moral peril and do not cooperate on the basis of wrongdoing and transgression." The Qur'an prohibited secret groups which scheme against others, particularly against the Prophet and his policies. These were the "hypocrites" and their fellow travelers. In al-Mujadilah: 8, the Qur'an reiterates this prohibition and then goes on to say: "O believers, if you hold private and secret meetings, do not plan on the basis of wrongdoing and transgression and disobedience of the Prophet, but plan on the basis of righteousness and warning each other against moral peril." My point in bringing up these verses is that the Qur'an envisages the Muslim community internally as a perfectly egalitarian, open society based on good will and cooperation, without elitism and the mentality that generates secret conspiracies. Of course, the anti-Islamic prohibitions against the community's political or other aspects of life in public, therefore forcing people to hold secret meetings, is condemned by the same verses, regardless of the purported justification. Secret meetings and such bans are in utter opposition to what the Qur'an envisions to be the internal life of the community. Quite apart from the fact that such bans are manifestly anti-Qur'anic, they are counterproductive and self-defeating as repeated experiences have shown. How many Muslim countries today can claim to be open societies? In the interest of communal solidarity, such measures may well be resorted to on a very temporary basis, but to make it permanent or semi-permanent is directly oposite to the Qur'an's stipulations.

The points we have made so far are (1) that the Qur'an has defined the role of the Muslim community to establish a certain kind of socialpolitical order and to balance extremes, (2) that the internal life and constitution of the Muslim society is to be re-

[4]The Qur'an 103:3
[5]The Qur'an 58:8

lentlessly egalitarian and open, unstained by elitism and no sec-
retiveness, and (3) that the internal life and conduct of society
pivots around mutual active good will and cooperation. The
Qur'an tolerates no distinction between one believer and another,
male and female, as to their equal participation in communal life.
In harmony with this vision, the Qur'an laid down the principle
of shura to guide the community's decision-making process. Unfortunately, there has grown, over the centuries, a terrible mis-
conception among Muslims concerning the nature of shura due
to misguided and misleading practices and structures adopted
from the outside without regard for the ethos of Islam. It is widely
held that shura means that one person, the ruler, consults men
who, in his judgment, are repositories of wisdom, with no obligation to implement their advice. First of all, this picture totally dis-
torts the structure shura presupposes. The Qur'an designates the
believers as "those whose affairs are decided by mutual consultation (*amruhum shura bainahum*)."[6] Shura, then, does not mean
that one person asks others for advice but, rather, *mutual advice*
through mutual discussions on an equal footing. This directly implies that the head or the chief executive cannot simply reject the
decision arrived at through shura.

The circumstances under which the classical doctrine of shura
and that of caliphate developed, producing the misconceptions
referred to just now, are essentially historical in nature and cannot be attributed to the Qur'an. So far as the prophetic period is
concerned, the mainstay of all authority was obviously the
Prophet himself, obedience to whose decisions was made binding
upon Muslims by the Qur'an. After him, and particularly during
the period of expansion of the domain of Islam to this very
phenomenon, shura was an informal affair in which the caliph
consulted an inner circle of leading companions of the Prophet.
Formalization or institutionalization of shura into anything like an
assembly was made impossible by the exigencies of continuous
wars, both because of the swiftness with which conquests were
made and the military nature of the problems. During the
Umayyad rule, these exigencies were not confined to external expansion but included internal politico-military consolidation as
well, since the entire Umayyad period witnessed incessant rebellions. The Umayyad rule altered the very character of the early
caliphate by imposing its own political logic to such an extent
that, far from facilitating communal participation, shura actually

---

[6]The Qur'an 42:38

became restricted to those who supported the regime. In fact, shura vanished into that very cliquing which the Qur'an condemned. It was the development of a structure which now supplied the link between the rulers and the ruled, only this link worked essentially from the top downward as opposed to shura which worked in reverse.

Nevertheless, the institution of *bai'ah*, or the oath of obeisance which legitimized the caliph's rule, continued to operate during the Umayyad rule. This period moreover saw the early development of Islamic law and legal theory by certain exceptionally gifted and pious individuals. The results of this legal creativity were subsequently implemented through the state judicial system during the 'Abbassid period, when legal schools were formed and consolidated. The classical Islamic theory of state also developed during the 'Abbassid rule. While the shi'ah evolved the doctrine of the infallible imam as the supreme religious guide and ruler — a doctrine close in spirit to (and probably also in line with) the ancient Iranian idea of divine kingship — the sunni theoreticians emphasized the elective nature of the caliph's office and that his function was restricted to acting as the chief executive of the community. Though they differed on how many people constitute an effective electoral college to appoint a caliph, they, nevertheless, held fast to the principle of election. The community could wrest its rights from the caliph in case he usurped them and would not listen to advice and warning and, indeed, he could also be legally deposed.

The people entrusted with electing and advising the caliph were generally influential and respected men within the community. These were called "people of loosening and binding (*ahl al-hall wal-'aqd*)." Since the principle of shura had been abandoned before it could develop into a self-sustaining institution, an appeal to the "people of loosening and binding" was the only alternative course available. Of course, what basically vitiated the sunni political institution was the insistence of the theoreticians — for which legitimation was sought from obviously concocted traditions and other dicta — that rebellion even against tyrannical rule was prohibited by Islam. Yet, the only real way to stop rebellions and the breakdown of law and order — the real reasons behind the sunni position — was to process the principle of shura into some practical form. This was not to be. We need not tarry further to consider later political developments, the age of the sultans, and the rise of empires in Islam in the later medieval period. What we have said should be enough to illustrate the yawning chasm between the ideals of the Qur'an and historical reality, where there was no direct participation whatsoever by the general community in the affairs of the state. We must now make some relevant comments on the contemporary scene.

Since about the mid-19th century, prominent leaders of reformist thought in Islam have argued that in order to implement Islam in the public sector, government must be established in accordance with the will of the people. One consideration that weighed particularly heavy with reformers like Jamal ad-Din al-Afghani was that without the participation of the people in the government, Muslim states could not become strong enough to withstand the pressures of the expanding West. Rulers without public support and confidence gave in easily to the demands of the Western powers. Second, for purposes of internal progress and development, without which Muslim states must also remain weak, the willing participation of the people was equally required. Namik Kemal, in his discussion of shura, raises valid questions about the legitimacy of rule without the approval of the people: if a person, Kemal asks, sets himself up as a judge merely on the strength of his own declaration and without appointment by a competent authority, his claim is regarded as invalid. Still, what about a person who declares himself to be a ruler, wages war and peace on behalf of people, and levies taxes on them without their consent?

Both of these considerations of progress and the legitimacy of the governing authority have fundamental Islamic relevance. The notion of progress is new while the idea of the general well-being and prosperity of the people is very old. The notion of progress is a modern differentiation of the idea of general well-being. As for the question of legitimacy, its importance had been fully realized by Muslim political theorists from the begining. Notwithstanding this, it is notorious how, pressed by the brute facts of historical realities, these theorists came to recognize the validity of "usurpation of power." Let us try to picture, if we can, the distance between the Qur'anic demand of "rule by mutual consultation *(amruhum shura bainahum)*" and the principle of usurpation of power. It is in this background that the real Islamic relevance and import of the principle of democracy insisted upon by al-Afghani and Namik Kemal is thrown into bold relief.

The most serious objection raised against the introduction of a democratic form of government by its opponents was that the general masses, being ignorant and unenlightened, could not elect the right kind of representatives, and that, the representatives since they themselves would probably be just ignorant, could not be expected to discern right from wrong and legislate correctly. This objection was, to my knowledge, first advanced by those Turks who sought to defend the imperial power of the Sultan against the protagonists of constitutionalism. To this objection, Namik Kemal gave a general reply that in the various districts of the Ottoman realm one can find people with enough wisdom and practical sense to carry on the business of the state successfully. A similar controversy occurred more recently between the Egyptian scholars 'Abd al-Hamid Mutawalli and Muhammad al-Ghazali. Al-Ghazali, replying to the tirade against democracy (in his *Mabda' al-Shura fi'l-Islam*), based upon the argument of the masses' ignorance insisted that the common man could decide if a certain war should be waged or not or if a certain proposed tax was fair or not.

The crux of the matter, however, came to the fore clearly in Muhammad Iqbal's critique of democracy as practiced in the West. Iqbal was undoubtedly a democrat even though in the recent debate in Pakistan, some people have attempted to underline Iqbal's hope or faith in some kind of a supreme leader or superman expressed in some of his poetic statements; yet, he bitterly denounced Western democratic systems. Now, the essence of his criticism is that the Western democratic societies aim only at accomplishing materialistic ends, and that the average Western man is devoid of any vision of a higher moral social order. This is precisely what Iqbal means by western secularism, which he perceived as developing from the very genesis of Christianity with its principle of "rendering unto Caesar what is Caesar's due and unto God what is God's due."

In the light of this, we are now ready to resume discussion of the point we started out with in this paper: the status and role of the Muslim ummah. We have just seen that Iqbal rejected Western democratic systems because of their lack of ethical and spiritual concerns. It is not their democratic forms and processes which are in error but their orientations and value systems. Now, this should not be the case with the Muslim ummah which, by its very constitution as well as by definition, is charged by the Qur'an with a certain global moral mission. It is tragic to see before our eyes the very logic of Iqbal's argument being twisted. All too often our leaders and thinkers state that because Western democracies are wrong in some fundamental way, democracy as a whole is wrong, and Islam does not approve of it. The fact is that if the Muslim ummah is just like other societies, including Western ones, then we must admit that the Muslim ummah does not exist since the task which the Qur'an has formulated rests squarely upon the shoulders of the ummah and not upon those of an elite. The mistake made by such leaders is to equate, surreptitiously and *e silentio*, the Muslim community and its task with other secular communities and their goals. Is this fair to the Muslim community and its responsibilities? The point I wish to make is that Muslims, instead of looking at other people and jumping to conclusions by drawing wrong analogies, must first look to Islam and to their own selves and then attempt to put their own house in order. Whether or not other societies have goals and ideals and, if they do, what these goals and ideals are, is not the Muslims' concern at this stage.

Despite all the above, there are apparent reasons why these mistaken analogies are drawn by so many of our leaders. The reason is that, although the Muslim community is explicitly charged with performing certain tasks and goals, Muslim masses, by and large, are said to be ignorant of these and, because of their lack of proper Islamic awareness, have become used to the condition of non-Muslim societies. I wish to remind the readers once again that if the Muslim community at large has lost the Islamic vision of life, then the Muslim ummah does not exist. If this is so, then no amount of self-styled political, religious, or intellectual elites can save the situation for Islam since the Qur'an has reposed its charge and its trust in the Muslim community alone. If there is hope, as the present writer firmly believes, then surely the first task that devolves upon the Muslim intellectuals and leaders is to reconstruct the ummah in an Islamically meaningful way. This task can neither be avoided nor delayed, except on pain of utterly defeating Islam.

It is obvious that this task cannot be achieved over night nor are we here to apportion blame for the derelict state of the ummah among various social segments, particularly governmental and religious leadership. It is a process that has been going on for many centuries, and, undoubtedly, the historical phenomenon of the fast expansion of Islam, without the necessary spiritual adjustments of the converts to the new faith, is responsible for it. If this task is undertaken in earnest, this will start a momentous remedial historical process in reverse. In the meantime, the participatory association of the ummah through directly ascertaining the will of the ummah in the political and legislative decisions affecting the life of the community can neither be rejected nor postponed. Those who advocate such a course of action are wittingly or unwittingly guilty of rendering Islam null and void, while God wishes to establish Islam throughout the world.

To recapitulate, let us ponder first of all the phrase *"amruhum"* in the Qur'anic verse *"wa amruhum shura bainahum."* "Amruhum" means their affairs – that is, the affair does not belong to an individual, a group or an elite, but it is *"their common affair"* and belongs to the community as a whole. Next, the command "shura bainahum," – that is, (their common affair) is to be decided by *their* common and mutual consultation and discussion — not by an individual or an elite whom they have neither elected nor sanctioned. What else is the Qur'an saying except that Muslims constitute an egalitarian and effective community or a brotherhood of equals?

THE THEORY OF VILAYAT-I FAQIH: ITS ORIGIN AND APPEARANCE IN SHI'ITE JURISTIC LITERATURE

Ahmad Moussavi

The revolution in Iran has brought into sharp focus the concepts of jurist's governance (*vilāyat-i faqih*), and *marja'-i taqlid* (locus of mass following). Both vilayat-i faqih and marja'-i taqlid, which often sound unfamiliar even to orthodox Muslims, are subdevelopments of the shi'ite imamate doctrine. The Islamic Revolution of Iran, as seen by its constitutional changes, is an actualization of the power that a supreme *mujtahid* should carry in his capacity as the imam's deputy.

This process has a religio-historic background that developed mainly in post-Safavid Iran. The immediate juridical background of the imam's deputyship is the establishment of the *usuli* position through 'Aqa Baqir Bihbihani (d. 1205 A.H.). The victory of the usuli 'ulema over the *akhbari* not only led to the formation of marja'-i taqlid, but helped Mulla Ahmad Naraqi (d. 1245 A.H.) to formulate the theory of jurists' governance in its general context.

The theory of vilayat-i faqih, in some respects, is the continuation of the imamate doctrine, for it performs the main functions of the imam's governance. It features the element of rational deputyship according to the people's choice, which differs with the imam's being appointed by God. However, the main factor — the individual rule of a charismatic leader — remained unchanged.

Both the imamate and the imam's deputyship are used to provide legitimacy for the ruling groups. The political approach of Islam is a part of its overall religious approach toward worldly matters. In this respect, the form of sovereignty which should represent God's sovereignty on this earth, as Iqbal put it, is only an effort to realize the spiritual in a human organization.

However, organizational development in Islam lagged behind its rich spiritual tradition. Even the pluralistic concepts of *jama'ah* (congregation), *bai'ah* (allegiance), and *shura* (council) have not yet been translated into formal political institutions. With the exception of *fityan* (Muslim brotherhood) groups, we cannot find any of the preceding Islamic concepts incorporated in Muslim political systems. On the other hand, we find the individualistic institutions, such as the appointed imam and his charismatic deputies, in shi'ite Islam.

However, the Qur'an's universal values, 'adl (justice) and qist (equity), are to judge the outcome of both collective and individualistic institutions. In examining the position of the 'ulema and maraji' and the shi'i doctrine of vilayat-i faqih, we will see how the notion of justice changes the whole legitimizing process in the case of imam-i 'ādil (just imam) and that of faqih-i 'ādil (just jurist).

Vilayat conveys several intricate meanings which are deeply tied to their history. Morphologically, it is derived from the Arabic wilāya the verbal noun of wāliyan: to be near and to have power over something. Technically, vilayat means rule, supremacy, or sovereignty. In another sense, vilayat (sometimes pronounced vilayat or walā') means friendship, sanctity, loyalty, or guardianship.

In shi'ite literature, vilayat implies allegiance to the rule of the imamas and recognition of their right to govern. A distinction has, over time, been made between general ('āmmah) and special (khassah) vilayat to distinguish between the general power (or right) of the imam and his legal authority as a qazi (judge) and guardian over special cases.

Since the end of the 12th century A.H., vilayat has come to mean the jurists' (fuqaha) authority, but its nature and scope has remained controversial. In this connection, Mulla Ahmad Naraqi (1185-1245 A.H.) was the leading jurist who employed vilayat for fuqaha' in terms of the mujtahids' supremacy over the twelver shi'ite community during the absence of the Imam of the Age. He identified the mujtahid as the most learned man whose search for a correct opinion has the value of speculative reasoning (zann). Naraqi considered this zann as a legal proof (dalil) since the gate of acquiring knowledge has been closed upon the disappearance of the 12th imam.[2]

On the other hand, a large number of 'ulema restricted mujtahids' responsibility to matters of guardianship and judgment. They argued that the general power belonged to the imam of the

---

[1]Muhammad Iqbal, The Reconstruction of Religions Thought in Islam (Lahore: Sheikh Mohammad Ashraf, 1958), p. 155.

[2]Mulla Ahmad Naraqi, 'Awa'id al-Ayyam (Qum: Maktabah Basirati, 1903), pp. 185-205.

age, and that during his absence nobody's authority could go beyond the right of other *mukallafs* (committed Muslims) except in terms of the delegation of power.[3]

Both the preceding approaches toward vilayat and mujtahid were the consequences of several historical and doctrinal processes which developed over several centuries. To deal successfully with the various applications of the vilayat-i faqih, it would be necessary to take a brief look at the four main phases of twelver shi'ite jurisprudence during which the 'ulema developed their authority on a doctrinal basis. The contemporary shi'ite 'ulema appear to be adopting a new classification for *ithna 'ashari* (twelver shi'ite) stages of jurisprudence. The first description of this classification was proposed by Professor Shahabi in the early 1930s, and was later approved in principle by the authoritative mujtahids of Qum such as the Ayatollah Buruhirdi (d. 1961).

According to Professor Shahabi, the following stages are significant in the last phase of twelver-shi'ite jurisprudence:

1. The beginning of Great Occultation of the 12th Imam (329 A.H.) up to the death of Shaykh-i Tusi (460 A.H.).
2. The period between the death of Shaykh-i Tusi to the rise of Ibn al-Mutahhar al-Hilli (d. 726 A.H.).
3. The stage between the rise of al-Hilli and 'Aqa Baqir Bihbihani (d. 1208 AH).
4. The period between 'Aqa Baqir Bihbihani to the present day.[4]

A. The Theme of Vilayat-i Faqih in the Early Stages

The first stage of twelver-shi'ite jurisprudence is known as the era of the traditionist (*muhaddithun*), whose great literary activities produced the first standard collections of the imams' traditions. Among them, three Muhammads: Kulayni (d. 329 A.H.), Shaykh-i Saduq (d. 381 A.H.), and Shaykh-i Tusi (d. 460 A.H.) are the most celebrated for their major collections of traditions and their contribution to Shi'ite jurisprudence:

In search for the theme of vilayat-i faqih within the juridical works of this period, one will soon note the fact that neither the term of vilayat-i faqih nor its tenor, as it is understood today, was

---

[3]The towering figure who maintained this view was Shaykh Murtaza Ansari (d. 1281 A.H.). See Murtaza Ansari, *al-Makasib* (Tabriz: Matba'ah Ittila'at, 1955), pp. 153-6.

[4]Mahmud Shahabi, *Advar-i Fiqh*, vol. 1 (Tehran: Danishgah-i 1961), p. 383.

employed in the early stages of twelver shi'ite history. Therefore, they must be traced back to their roots in the office of imams' deputies (nuvvab) and judges (qazis).

1) Nuvvab-i Imam (The Imams' Deputies): The office of the imam's deputy is created by delegating some of the imam's power to an ordinary mukallaf. This delegation may be done by the imam or by a self-claimed agency and popular recognition. Since the function of the imamate depends on the imam himself, theoretically there is no permanent office of na'ib-i imam, nor is there a division of the imam's duties. However, we may distinguish four types of na'ib-i imam which function in the shi'ite community.

First, there is the vakil (agent of the imam). He is a delegated agent who wields the imam's personal power in its legal sense. Most of the twelve imams had agents appointed to handle their financial affairs. The vakil was considered an agent mainly for receiving goods and money.

Second, there exists the na'ib-i khass (special deputy). Historically, this particular delegation of power was limited to four persons who bore the title of nuvvab-i khassa (special deputies) or sufara' (ambassadors) during the Lesser Occultation of the 12th imam (260-329 A.H.). The function of special deputies was broader than that of the vakil, since they used to deliver the imam's own handwritten ordinances (tawqi'at). The contents of these ordinances, however, delegate more of the imam's political or even juridical authority to the ambassadors. Rather, most of the 49 items of tawqi'at which Shaykh-i Saduq collected in his Ikmal ud-Din[5] and many of the 28 dispatches quoted by Shaykh-i Tusi[6] are concerned with financial matters between the imam's special deputies and his false vicegerents, who numbered at least seven according to Majlisi (d. 1111 A.H.).[7]

The third type is the na'ib-i 'am (general deputy). This applies to the 'ulema of each age who attain the rank of mujtahids and, in the absence of 'ulema, the 'udul-i Mu'minin (just Muslims). The scope of this duty, according to the prevalent view of the twelver shi'ites, is limited to the vilayat-i khassa, which includes qaza'

---

[5]Muhammad ibn 'Ali ibn Babuya Shaykh-i Saduq, Ikmal al-Din wal-Itmam l-Ni'mah, vol. 2, ed. M. B. Kamara'i (Tehran: Islamiyyah, 1960), pp. 159-202.

[6]Abu Ja'far Muhammad ibn Hasan, Shaykh-i Tusi, Kitab al-Ghaybah. (Najaf: Matba'a an-Nu'man, 1966), pp. 172-199.

[7]Muhammad Baqir Majlisi, Bihar al-Anwar, vol. 13, tr. 'Ali Davani (Tehran: Muhammadi, 1965), pp. 517 538.

(judgment) and matters of custody. It is important to note that the idea behind na'ib-i 'ām is that the imam's vilayat, in special cases such as *jihad and khums*, is exposed to general agency. Since the mujtahids are publicly recognized as being qualified, they are first in authority to carry out the imam's powers.

The final type of na'ib is the *na'ib fi umur al-'ämmah* (deputy of public affairs). This covers those mujtahids who claimed for themselves the vilayat-i 'āmmah or the complete delegation of the imam's power during his absence. This kind of na'ib over public affairs, which is a post-Safavid development, should not be mistaken for the na'ib-i 'ām, which can be traced to the earlier juridical periods.

Among the preceding forms of deputship, only the first and second types can be found during the first juridical stage. The juridical work at this time was mainly concerned with the imam and his infallibility, rather than with his actual vicegerents who must fulfill the imam's political functions. In fact, the juridical process during this phase, while it fostered the notion of *ghaybat*, did not provide any concept other than *intizar* (patient expectancy for salvation) for the days after the great occultation. Of course, the idea of intizar suited the pluralistic character of the religious developments of the 4th century A.H. This notion could tolerate the existing regime without losing the aspiration for a change for the better.

2) Jurists as Judges: The position of the qazi, from the twelver-shi'ite viewpoint, seems well-established for the fuqaha'.[8] Its justification resides mainly in the bulk of traditions which Shaykh-i Saduq has cited from the imams. The only essential twelver-shi'ite source before Saduq belongs to Kulayni, who quoted the celebrated tradition on the authority of Ibn Hanzalah from Ja'far as-Sadiq. The imam directed his followers not to present their cases to *tāghūt* (wrongdoing authorities), but rather to look for whoever recites the imam's traditions.[9]

It is remarkable that Kulayni, who was a contemporary of the imam's special deputies during the lesser occultation, did not mention as many *tawqi's* and proofs of the 12th Imam as Saduq

---

[8]Hakim Muhsin Tabataba'i, *Mustamsak al-Urwah al-Wathqah*, vol. 1 (Najaf: 'il-miyyah, 1957), pp. 64-65.

[9]Muhammad ibn Ya'qub Kulayni, *al-Usul min al-Kafi*, vol. 1, ed. M. B. Kamara'i (Tehran: Islamiyyah, 1962), p. 113.

did only one generation later. His reference to the imam's tawqi'at is limited to three letters concerning financial affairs.[10] Even in the case of ghaybat, he has mainly based himself on the 6th Imam, and not his contemporary imam. It is quite common in shi'ite literature to gain legitimacy for a new notion by ascribing it to the previous imams, rather than the contemporary ones.

B. The Establishment of the Usuli School and the Position of Marja'iyyat-i Taqlid

Usul implies the doctrine of the "principles" of Muslim jurisprudence, and *'ilm al-usul* is generally considered as the science of proofs which leads to the establishment of legal standards. The proofs, according to twelver shi'ites, are: the Qur'an, the traditions of the Prophet and the imams, ijma', and *'aql*. Ijma', according to twelver shi'ites, is the unanimous consent of the Muslim community which contains the word of an infallible imam. Ijma', because it represents the imam's opinion, is considered to be proof.[11] 'Aql may be translated as intellect, but technically, in shi'ite jurisprudence, it is confined to four practical principles: *bara'at* (immunity), *ihtiyat* (precaution), *takhyir* (selection), and *istishab* (continuity in the previous state).[12] All these principles should be employed by mujtahids only when other religious proofs are not applicable. In fact, these principles are no more than speculative reasoning. Sharing juristic speculation with explicit proofs was objected to by the akhbari, another branch of the shi'ite school.

In contrast to the usuli, the akhbari rely primarily on the traditions of the Prophet and imams as the source of religious knowledge. Opposing usuli and akhbari currents were apparent in twelver shi'ism from its very beginning, although it multiplied in the course of time.

In the first juridical period (4th and 5th centuries Hijrah) the twelver jurists of the Iraqi school — Shaykh-i Saduq, Shaykh-i Mufid, and Sharif-i Murtaza — espoused a combined usuli and *kalami* position by adopting Mu'tazali theological principles. It was Shaykh-i Tusi, however, who developed a distinctive methodology in shi'ite jurisprudence. Moreover, he wrote 'Uddat

---

[10]See Ibn Babuya Saduq, *Ikmal al Din*, vol. 2, pp.
[11]Mahmud Shahabi, *Taqrirat-i Usul* p. 114 15.
[12]*Ibid.*, pp. 117-120.

al-Usul, which is considered to be the first comprehensive book on shi'ite principles of jurisprudence.[13]

It should be mentioned here that, to some extent, shi'ite jurists borrowed Mu'tazali and Shaf'i principles to systematize the twelver jurisprudence. For example, in the section dealing with the validity of solitary tradition (*hujiyyat-i khabar-i vahid*), the Shaf'i influence is quite evident.

The second wave of the usuli trend, which subsequently shaped the third juridical stage, occurred during the Mongol period. In this stage, the concept of ijtihad was revived with a new meaning. According to Ayatollah Mutahhari, Ibn al-Mutahhar al-Hilli was probably the first shi'ite jurist who used the term of mujtahid in the sense of one who deduces a religious ordinance on the basis of the authentic shari'ah arguments.[14]

Ayatollah Mutahhari said that in the early periods, the word ijtihad was hated by twelver-shi'ite jurists because it was associated with the meaning of *ijtihad al-ra'y* (giving personal opinion on the basis of *qiyas, istihsan and istislah*, which shi'ites do not recognize). From the 5th century onward, when sunni scholars such as al-Ghazzali restricted ijtihad to the deduction of juridical ordinance on the basis of shari'ah sources, the twelvers were ready to accept ijtihad.[15]

Other prominent jurists, Muhaqqiq-i Hilli, Ibn Makki and Shahid-i Thani, who lived at the same time and after Ibn al-Mutahhar, discussed the question of ijtihad in this new sense. Even so, the one who most clearly articulated the new ithna 'ashari perception of ijtihad and consequently *taqlid* was Shaykh Hasan 'Amili (d. 1011 A.H.), the author of the celebrated book *Ma'alim al-usul*. The usuli trend stopped flourishing in the 11th

---

[13]Abdul-Qasim Gurji, "Shaykh-i Tusi va 'Uddat al-Usul," *Hizara-yi Shaykh-i Tusi*, vol. 2, ed. Davani (Qum: Dar al-Tabligh Islamic), pp. 65-75.

[14]Murtaza Mutaharri, "Ijtihad dar Islam," *Bahsi dar-bar-yi Marja'iyyat-* (Tehran: Shirkat-i Intisharat, 1962), p. 42.

[15]Ayatollah Mutahhari took a contradictory view of ijtihad in the millenium anniversary celebrations for Shaykh-i Tusi in March 1970. Responding to Dr. Charles Adams, who had compared Shaykh-i Tusi's contribution to the methodology of shi'ite jurisprudence with a Shaf'i (d. 204 A.H.), Ayatollah Mutahhari claimed that shi'ites used to employ ijtihad even in the presence of the imams. He did not elaborate on what type of ijtihad he was referring to; however, it is understood from his account that juridical ijtihad which rates as proof (hujjah) is not included. See 'Ali Davani, *Hizara yi Shaykh-i Tusi*, vol. 2 pp. 29-48.

century Hijrah because of the akhbari resurgence through Mulla Amin Astrabadi (d. 1033 A.H.). Time, however, was on the usuli side, thanks to the lasting concealment of the Imam of the Age and the growing need for a wider interpretation of the shari'ah sources.

The emergence of a pragmatic jurist, 'Aqa Baqir Bihbihani (1118-1205 A.H.), in Karbala not only helped the usuli school reestablish itself, but gave it an additional position, marja' iyyat-i taqlid. Bihbihani, who enjoys the title of founder (mu'assis) of a new stage in twelver-shi'ite jurisprudence, was never considered a brilliant scholar like Ibn al-Mutahhar or Shahid-i Thani. His significance lies in his practical manner in winning popular support against the akhbari and eliminating them in Iran and Iraq. In pre-Qajar periods, the question of akhbarism was a matter of tendency and style, but Bihbihani, by refuting the akhbari, managed to outlaw them as heretics.

Bihbihani's lifelong argument with his rival, Shaykh Yusuf Bahrayni (d. 1172 A.H.), centered on the validity of the mujtahids' speculative opinion after the gate of acquiring knowledge had been closed by the disappearance of the 12th imam. What Bihbihani achieved was not merely the validity of the juristic ijtihad, but the appeal to follow a figurehead mujtahid. The religious circumstances of the time, however, helped Bihbihani and his disciples elevate their standing from a juridical basis to the locus of a mass following (marja'-i taqlid). It was then that the theory of vilayat-i faqih was clearly established by Bihbihani's pupil, Mulla Ahmad Naraqi (d. 1245 A.H.).

The first mujtahid who historically carried the title of marja' was Hajj Shaykh Muhammad Hasan Isfahani Najafi (d. 1266 A.H.). It must be stated that Isfahani, although a good author, had no particular distinction from the previous mujtahids. His title of marja' indicates the significance of the juridical process toward the supremacy of a single mujtahid over the shi'ite mukallafs, as he happened to live at the right time. A question may come to mind as to why none of Isfahani's contemporary mujtahids, such as Nararqi, enjoyed the title of absolute marja' as the former did for six years.

Piety and intellectual qualifications were not the only prerequis-

---

[16]'Aqa Baqi Bihbihani, Risalat al-Ijtihad wal-Akhbar, (Manuscript, Iran, 1895), pp. 1-20.

ites for this title. The most important element was the ability of the marja' to pay the students' bread money. To do so, the marja' had to reside in the religious cities such as Najaf and Qum. In addition, he had to be able to draw money in terms of *sahm-i imam*, khums, zakat, and awqaf. Therefore, marja'iyyat carried with it some sort of formalities which has little to do with being the most learned jurist.

It is illogical to assume that the early great jurists, such as Kulayni, were primarily marja' or even mujtahid,[17] since the concept of marja'iyyat-i taqlid had never been brought up in pre-Qajar times. Even the notion of ijtihad in its new shi'ite sense did not precede the days of Ibn al-Mutahhar al-Hilli. In the early juridical phases, the doctrine of imam and its necessity and infallibility were so prevalent that none of the fallible mukallaf (even a learned one) could claim legal validity for his opinion. Moreover, the concealment of the 12th Imam, according to the tone of early twelver-shi'ite works, was not expected to be long enough for developing an alternative solution during his absence.

C. The Government Legitimizing Process from the Juridical Point of View

The limited scope of this work does not permit going into the complex problem of governmental legitimacy within the twelver shi'ite community. However, since the legitimacy crisis of post-Safavid Iran is one of the major contributing factors to the evolution of vilayat-i faqih, some aspects of this issue will be briefly discussed.

There are three basic approaches in modern scholarship regarding state legitimacy or illegitimacy in a twelver-shi'ite society. Algar Keddie and, to some extent, Lambton, who are mainly concerned with Qajar literature, present a view typical of the Qajar's usuli school. According to them, the twelver-shi'ite doctrine denies the legitimacy of any state, even a twelver one, pending the return of the Imam of the Age.[18] During his absence, the 'ulema, in a limited sense, are the intermediaries between the community and the imam, and enjoy some of his authority.[19]

---

[17]For example, see Ha'iri 'Abd al-Hadi, *Shi'ism and Constitutionalism*, Ph.D. dissertation, Institute of Islamic Studies, McGill, Montreal, 1973), pp. 124-28.

[18]Nikki Keddi, "The Roots of the 'Ulama's Power in Modern Iran," *in Scholars, Saints and Sufis: Muslim Religious Institutions since 1500* (Berkely, 1972), p. 212.

[19]*Hamid Algar, Religion and State,* p. 5.

These three scholars have based their understanding primarily on the stories about the 'ulema, rather than on the 'ulema's own books. However, they fail to place enough importance on the practical methods of shi'ite jurisprudence such as *asl al-ibaha* (permissiveness), *asl al-sihha* (correctness), and *izn-i saltanat* (permission of sovereignty); these methods have been elaborated on by the 'ulema to bridge the gap between religious ideals and practical needs during the Qajar period.

The second approach views the theory of occultation as a legitimizing process not for the 'ulema but for secular powers. Its leading figure, Sa'id Amir Arjomand, was strongly opposed to the first approach. However, before him, the scholar Joseph Eliash arrived at a similar conclusion by investigating the non-delegation of the imam's authority in some of the twelver-shi'ite early works, especially in Kulayni's *al-Kafi*:

> Applied to an ithna 'ashari-shi'i community living in this period, namely between 329/940 and the end of time, the ithna 'ashari-shi'i doctrine of the imamate secularizes its political institution, demands humanization of both the legislative body of such a community and the very process of legislation sanctioning an interpretation of justice in terms of welfare, based on and derived from the welfare of the individual and not the interest of any institution, either religious or political.[20]

Eliash, nevertheless, does not explain how and why shi'ites idealized and then humanized the government, and how the whole problem of legitimacy has been dealt with up to the present day.

Amir Arjomand applies the analysis of the sociology of religion to the problem of legitimate domination in shi'ite Iran. Referring to Hodgson's exposition of early imamate history, he states that the *de facto* depoliticization of the imamate was concomitant with the sectarian reorientation of early shi'ism, which began with the 5th Imam and became firmly established by the Imam Ja'far as-Sadiq.[21] The doctrine of ghaybah, which was a solution to the succession problem in the imamate crisis, following the death of the 11th Imam, accentuated the divorce between the imamate

[20]Joseph Eliash, "The Ithna 'Ashari Juristic Theory of Political and Legal Autjority," *Studia Islamica*, vol. 29, (1969):p. 28.

[21]M. G. S. Hodgson, "How Did the Early Shi'ah Become Sectarian?" quoted by Said Amir Arjomand in: "Legitimate Domination in Shi'i Iran," *Archives Europeans Sociologie XX p. 64.*

and political rule.[22]

Moreover, the practices of *taqiyyah* (dissimilation of faith to assure survival) and the sufficiency of intention to enjoin the good (*amr bi al-ma'ruf*) and prohibit the evil (*nahi 'an al-munkar*) in cases of potential danger are considered as the deemphasizing process on the Islamic political ethic. Nonetheless, the practice of the Imami shi'ites was considered to be consistent with the implicit secularization of political authority. From the time of the sect's formation, many Imamis entered the service of rulers and achieved great prominence.[23] Amir Arjomand concludes his discussion with the following interesting remarks:

> Strictly speaking, there existed no shi'ite theory of government by the end of the eighteenth century. With the modification of the notion of imamate through successive ages, and as a consequence of the shi'ite belief in the prolonged occultation of the Imam of the Age, the imamate lost all connotation of actual political rule and became a topic not of legal theory but of theology. shi'ism came to consider temporal rule as profane and a matter of doctrinal indifference. Because of its lack of concern with temporal rule, the shi'ite religion allowed the prevalence of the normatively autonomous principles of legitimacy [to be] incorporated in the Persian theory of kingship.
>
> What is, however, of far greater interest is the crucial consequence of the transformation of the political notion of imamate into a theological one. This transformation meant that the imamate became a topic not of jurisprudence but of theology; the prospects for the development of a shi'ite political theory and of shi'ite public law were adversely affected.[24]

The problem with this approach is that it supports something in theory, while in reality its opposite has been proven. It fails to see that the *de facto* depoliticizing function of the imamate theories — ghaybat, taqiyyah — was changed throughout both popular extremist religiosity (*ghali* and sufi developments), and juridical advances toward the imam's political authority in terms of his rational deputies. Amir Arjomand's remarks concerning the

---

[22]*Ibid.*

[23]Said Amir Arjomand: "Legitimate Domination in Shi'i Iran."

[24]*Ibid.*, p. 108.

early period of imamate seem correct. It was then that the imamate, which was never a subject of jurisprudence, became a topic of theology. In the Mongol and post-Mongol periods, one is faced with imamate movements rather than with its theological development. The political themes of these movements cannot be measured by an abstract criterion like the depoliticization function of occultation — a theory of the early stage whose function was diversified over time.

In an attempt to find a more compatible approach to the problem of state legitimacy in a twelver-shi'ite community, one comes across the socialist scholarship of Petrushevski in his *Islam in Iran*. It can be inferred from his account that shi'ism was essentially a vehicle for religious expression by popular political movements in Islamic territories. The shi'ite state acquired legitimacy through the support of their class base[25] in the form of extremist religious movements, and not in the form of juridical theories which were open to diverse interpretation.[26] Petrushevski observes that after the Safavids' victory in Iran, shi'ism diversified its ghali-sufi characteristics in order to become an established base for Safavid feudalism. Therefore, it gave up its popular legitimacy in favor of the ruling class.[27]Socialist scholarship, however does not concern itself with the complicated rhetoric of the depoliticizing or secularizing processes because it considers all imamate developments as basically economic-political factors which have acquired religious expression.

Let us now turn to the shi'ite 'ulema's perception of governmental legitimacy. Twelver-shi'ite jurists have approached this issue on two levels: (1) they idealized the imam's legitimate government and, from the Qajar period onwards, the jurists' vilayat; and (2) they dealt with the ruling government in the absence of the Imam of the Age. Keeping faith in the idealized imam's rule, the twelver shi'ite 'ulema developed the following formulas to legitimize the ruling government:

1) **Sultan-i 'Adil (The Just Government):** This concept developed mainly in pre-Safavid times. Shaykh-i Tusi said: "The authority given by a just sultan, who rules properly, enjoins good and prohibits evil, is either recommendable or obligatory, but carrying

---

[25]Ilia Pavlovich Petrushevski, *Islam dar Iran*, tr. Karim Kishavarz (Tehran: Institut-i Piyam, 1971), Chapters 10 and 13.

[26]*Ibid.*, p. 396.

[27]Shaykh-i Tusi, *An-Nahayah*, tr. M.B. Sabzavari (Tehran: Danishgah-i, 1954), p. 239.

the authority of tyrannical governments is optional."[28] Ideas similar to Shaykh-i Tusi's are found in Shaykh-i Mufid's *al-Muqni*, Muhaqqiq Hilli's *Sharayi' al-Islam*, Ibn al-Mutahhar's *Tahrir*, Shahid-i Thani's *Masalik al-Afham*, and Majlisi's *Haq al-Yaqin*.[29] The idea of governmental service develops in Ibn al-Mutahhar's works since he uses the term "legitimate government" (*sultan al-haqq*) instead of *sultan al-'ādil*.[30]

2) Izn-i Vilāyat (Allowance of Authority): This formula flourished substantially during the Qajar period. However, it had existed to a limited extent and on the basis of the imam's permission before the Safavid era. Afterwards, the 'ulema assumed this duty since some of the Qajar kings frequently requested their permission. Muhaqqiq-e Hilli, in his discussion on just government, said that it would be obligatory to accept the just goverment's authority if it was originally assigned by the imam.[31] The tone of his statement indicates that access to the imam's permission in Hilli's days was possible.

In fact, having contact or communication with the Imam of the Age (the source of legitimacy) was not as difficult as Western scholarship believed. Contact and communication was often carried out through dreams, inspirations, or mystical experiences, even in the form of rumors. It is known that there were publicly accepted contacts claimed by the Four Special Deputies and the Safavids' Shaykhs; now may be added a list of 'ulema such as Muqqadis-i Ardabili, Shaykh Murtaza Ansari, and Ayatollah Khomeini whose rumored contacts with the imam were publically accepted. In the case of Ayatollah Khomeini, modern-day Iran witnesses that, parallel to his juridical build-up of vilayat-i faqih, his rumored contact with the Imam of the Age for obtaining permission (especially on the eve of revolution of February 10th, 1978) was a major contributing factor to his mass legitimacy.

3) Asl al-Ibahah (Permissiveness) and Asl as-Sihhah (Soundness): These are usuli juridical methods of legitimizing decisions in the absence of a specific religious ordinance (*hukm-i shar'.*) or legal proof (*dalil*). These methods were largely applied to goverments' legitimacy during the Qajar period. Asl al-ibahah juridically implies the permissibility of allowed practices which are

---

[28]Hadar 'Ali Qalamdaran, *Hukumat-i dar Islam*. (Tehran: Matba'ati Yi Islama'ilian, 1965), pp. 404-407.

[29]Ibn al-Mutahhar al-Hilli, *Tahrir al-Ahkam* (Tehran: n.p., 1895), p. 163.

[30]Muhaqqiq-i Hilli, *Sharayi' al-Islam*. (Tehran, n.d.), p. 97.

[31]Haydar 'Ali Qalamdaran, pp. 422-28.

often used by mujtahids to legalize their own opinions.

Asl as-sihhah implies the correctness of Muslim practices unless proven otherwise. This presumption was employed mainly to validate ambiguous cases since some jurists perceived the government to be such a case.

Many twelver jurists referred to the imams' relations with their contemporary governments as an example of how they should deal with government. Historically, many shi'ite imams accepted governmental awards, which implies a kind of recognition. According to Twelver sources, Imam Hasan received Mu'awiyah's donation after his compromise; Imam Reza became Ma'mun's crown prince; Imam Musa ibn Ja'far called Harun ar-Rashid *Emir al-Mu'minin* (Commander of the Believers) while receiving his rewards, Imam Ja'far as-Sadiq both accepted Davvaniqi's award and denounced him.[32] Some of the shi'ite 'ulema, such as Ibn al-Mutahhar al-Hilli, Shaykh 'Ali Karaki, and Majlisi, sided with a positive interpretation of the imam's traditions. Some others, like Shahid-i Aval, treated these traditions as exceptional cases which may be based on taqiyyah and the imam's own policy. Therefore, the imam's actions do not set patterns for the 'ulema and ordinary mukallafs.[33]

4) Darurat (Exigency): Reliance on the exigencies of practical politics for legitimizing the government was employed during the early period of imamate history. The roots of this can be traced back to the famous tradition of Imam 'Ali in the Saffayn war, when he heard the cry of the Kharijite that "only gives the verdict" and said:

> The sentence is right but what (they think) it means is wrong. It is true that verdict lies only with Allah, but these people say that the function of governance is only for Allah. The fact is that there is no escape for men from the ruler, good or bad. The faithful persons perform good acts in his rule while the unfaithful enjoy worldly benefits in it. Through the ruler, tax is collected, the enemy is fought, roadways are protected, and the right of the weak is taken from the strong till the virtuous enjoys peace and the wrongdoer is corrected.[34]

---

[32]Muhammad Tunakabuni, pp. 346 52.

[33]Imam 'Ali, *Nahj al-Balagha*. Collected by Sharif-i Qazi, tr. Mufti Ja'far Hussain (Qum: Barrasihyi Islami, 1975), p. 199.

[34]Kulayni, *Usul al-Kafi*, vol. 2 (Tehran: Islamiyya, 1962), p. 194.

Another tradition has been quoted from Imam Ja'far as-Sadiq in the story of Ibrahim, who referred to the necessity of government.[35] However, this idea did not develop in shi'ite jurisprudence, whereas the notion of the Imam's return (raj'ah) and its salvationary mission did.

Last, the distinction between shari'ah (religious law) and 'urf (common law) covers all customary and practical rules which are not explicitly mentioned in the shari'ah. Lacking any stipulation in the shari'ah, most governmental affairs in the twelver-shi'ite community were subjected to 'urf. From the Safavid period onwards, 'urf courts were administered by local authorities. Although 'urf jurisdiction frequently overlapped with shari'ah, the distinction between these two facilitated the actual recognition of the state authorities, hakim-i 'urf (the judge of 'urf).

Sir John Malcolm has given a description of 'urf vis-a-vis shari'ah in his study on the contemporary Qajar period. He suggested that native traditions and customary practices were incorporated in 'urf.[36] However, 'urf appears to be a parallel development to shari'ah. On the other hand, the 'ulema seemed to rely on 'urf as a scapegoat in obscure cases. Some pious mujtahids tended to approach all political affairs as non-shar'i 'urf matters. In the Iranian Constitution of 1906, however, the formal separation of shari'ah from 'urf was utilized as a means to legitimize all state institutions.[37]

In light of the preceding considerations, one may add here that the problem of state legitimacy in the twelver-shi'ite society of Iran is a part of its overall socio political problem as depicted in its messianic form of religiosity. In other words, the imamate doctrine of the 12th Imam's (Mehdi) legitimate government is based on the common conviction of his just behavior and salvationary mission, of which the society is in pressing need. Although colored by legends and mystical interpretations, the social functions of Imam Mehdi remain the most legitimizing factor of his government. As to the doctrinal base, it has already been seen how the notion of justice brought legitimacy for sultan-i 'ādil, and how many juridical devices were formulated over time to meet the community's practical needs.

Thus, isolating the imamate doctrine of government in its religi-

---

[35]John Malcolm, Tarikh-i Iran, tr. Mirza Haydar (Tehran, 1886), p. 154.
[36]Iranian Constitution of 1906, Articles 71 & 73.
[37]Muhammad Tunakabuni, Qisas al-'Ulema, p. 191.

ous aspect from its social structure, as most Western scholars did, leads to incompatible conclusions. There is no isolated source of legitimacy bestowed upon the imam or his nuvvab. The roots of the 'ulema's legitimacy in Iran may not be fully understood in its religious context of na'ib-i imam, unless it is juxtaposed with the justice and welfare function of the imam. Historically, the concept of na'ib-i imam did not provide legitimacy for a sizable number of learned mujtahids who did not support social justice or had sided with the oppressive ruling governments.

It must be noticed, however, that the doctrinal legitimation of the 'ulema's power in Iran was not realized until it coincided with the political weakness of the Qajar shi'ite rulers. Although the tradition of feudalist monarchy was deeply rooted in Iran, the government faced a legitimacy crisis after the fall of the Safavid Imamzadih.* Nadir Shah-i Afshar (d. 1160 A.H.), who reunited Iran under his administration, could not officially assume the rule before having it approved by a national assembly. For the first time in Iranian history, heads of tribes, along with *mullas*, were summoned to Dasht-i Mughan (1149 A.H.) to proclaim the legitimacy of a new monarch.

Nadir's successor, Karim Khan-i Zand, was never considered a king; he gave himself the title of *vakil al-ra'aya*, the people's deputy. The event of Dasht-i Mughan and the formula *vakil al-ru'aya* indicate that, in the absence of a religious or strong tribal legitimacy, the actual ruler of a shi'ite community needs something extra in order to prolong his sovereignty. However, the vast tribal heritage of the Qajar, coupled with the military talent of Agha Muhammad Shah (d. 1211 A.H.), brought the initial tribal basis of the Persian feudalist monarchy back to normal. Soon after him, in the absence of a capable leadership, the inadequacy of the Qajar tribal legitimacy surfaced. Agha Muhammad Shah's successor, Fath 'Ali Shah (d. 1248 A.H.) turned to religious charismatic figures in order to gain their support.

From the very beginning of his reign, Fath 'Ali Shah based his legitimacy on religious rather than tribal grounds. He asked Shaykh Ja'far Najafi, the leading mujtahid of 'atabat, to give him izn-i saltanat – that is, to permit him to mount the throne and appoint the Shah as his deputy. [38] This type of juridical accommodation, which was implemented during Fath 'Ali Shah's reign, has no precedent in shi'ite Iran. Fath 'Ali Shah was not content with Shaykh Ja'far Najafi's permission, nor with izn-i saltanat. In

---

* The Safavid rulers enjoyed a religious sanction of both Sufi and shi'ite origins.

addition to acquiring permission from various sources, he affiliated himself fraternally with a sizable number of 'ulema.

It would be wrong, however, to conclude that the Shah's legitimacy was dependent upon the 'ulema's approval. Of course, it was a major contributing factor, but the ultimate authority still lay in its tribal feudalist elements. For example, when the Shah's devotion was directed toward Sufi charisma during the reign of Fath 'Ali Shah's successor, Muhammad Shah (d. 1264 A.H.), the Shah's legitimacy was not seriously affected. The point is that Fath 'Ali Shah's religious attitude not only helped enhance the 'ulema's power, but it also contributed to a number of juridical developments such as the formation of the doctrine of vilayat-i faqih through Mullah Ahmad Naraqi.

Prophet Muhammad, upon whom be peace, Muslims from the earliest times have been guided in determining the criteria for true jihad. Jihad is not merely an end in itself but is, if conducted truly in the way of Allah, the first tool for the maintenance of the Islamic community and the establishment of an Islamic state.

INDEX

also, jurist(s).
Faqih-i 'ādil (just jurist), 98
al-Fārābi, 40
Fard 'ayn (individual duty), 58, 67
Fard kifayah (collective duty), 58, 67
al-Fāruqi, Isma'il R., 7
Fātimah (Prophet's daughter), 53
Financial administration, 17
Fiqh (jurisprudence), 25, 52; see also Islamic law and jurisprudence.
Fisq (immoral behavior), 74, 76
Fityan, 97

al-Ghalabah (military force), 72
Ghayabat (occultation), 101, 102, 106, 107
al-Ghazali, Muhammad, 94
al-Ghazzali, 8, 45, 63, 65, 66, 68, 69, 70, 73, 80, 103
Gibb, H.A.R., 74
Gilani, I'jaz Shafi, 14
Goliath, 143
Government, 4, 14, 36, 51, 61, 69, 80, 82, 93, 105, 108, 109, 111; Imamate doctrine of, 111, Islamic form of, 4, 14; just, 109; legitimacy of, 105, 109, 111; legitimacy crisis of, 105, 112; necessity of, 111.
Governmental organizations, 15
Group interests, 28
Group theory, 1, 2
Gurji, 'Abdul-Qasim, 103

al-Hadd, 49, 75

al-Hadīd, ibn Abi, 76
Hadîth, 5, 16, 25, 32, 56, 133, 134, 137, 139, 141, 142, 143, 145, 146
Hajj (pilgrimage), 87
Hakim-i 'urf (common law judge), 111
Hanafiyyah, 75
Hanbali school, 62
Haq al-Yaqin, 109
Harun, A., 72
Harun ar-Rashid, 110
Hasan ibn 'Ali, 77
Hasan, Ibrahim Hasan, 52, 58, 72
Hayder, Mirza, 111
Hegel, Friedrich, 51
Heraclitus, 27
Hijrah (migration), 37, 104, 138, 145
al-Hilli, ibn al Mutahhar, 99, 103, 105, 109, 110
Hilmi, M., 68
Hizballah (party of God), 38
Hobbes, Thomas, 51
Hodgson, M.G.S., 106
Holocaust, 31
Holy war, 133; see also jihad
Hourani, G.F., 122
Hudaibiyyah, 76
Hudayfah, 41
Hujja (proof), 80, 103, 123
Hujiyat-i khabar-i vahid (validity of solitary tradition), 103
al-Hukkam (rules), 60
Hukm-i shar'i (religious ordinance), 109
Human rights, 21, 22, 27, 28, 33, 48, 84; see also, civil rights
Hunain (battle of), 144
Huququl 'ibad (rights of people), 48, 55
Huquq ullah (rights of God), 48
Ibish, Yusuf, 54, 57, 62, 63, 64, 66, 67, 68, 69, 70, 71, 72, 76

Ibn 'Abd al-Hakam, 77
Ibn Abi Najih, 142
Ibn 'Aqil, 58
Ibn 'Atiyyah, 77
Ibn Hanbal, 81
Ibn Hanzalah, 101
Ibn Hazm, 72, 75, 76

156

Index

Legislative activity in Islam, 35, 49
Legislative Function(s), 61
Legislative Process, 82
Legislature, 28, 35, 36, 39, 49, 50; in Islamic state, 49, 81
Legitimacy, 63, 67, 93, 106, 108, 112, 113, 127, 128, 129; crisis of, 105, 112; of government, 105, 109, 111; popular, 108; principles of, 107; sources of, 109, 112; of state, 108, 111; tribal, 112; of 'ulema, 112
Legitimate domination (in shi'ism), 106
Lerner, Daniel, 20
Locke, John, 7, 51

Majlis (assembly), 81
Majlisi, Muhammad Bagir, 100, 109, 110
Makkah, 39, 68, 87, 139, 144
Makkan tribes, 116
Malcolm, Sir John, 111
Malik, Imam, 25, 54
Maliki Juristic school, 54
Mamelukes, 74
Ma'mun, 110
Managerial behavior, 15
Marja'-i taqlīd (locus of mass following), 10, 11, 97, 98, 102, 104, 105; absolute, 104; juridical basis of, 104; see also, vilāyat-i faqih.
Marwan, 44
Marwanids, 65
Marx, karl, 35
Marxist-Leninism, 27, 29
Marxist ideology, 48
al-Maslah (public interest), 65
Mass media, 4

Maududi, Abul A'la, 6, 13, 19, 134, 139
al-Mawardi, Abūl Hasan 'Ali, 6, 26, 45, 53, 55, 56, 57, 58,

59, 64, 66, 67, 69, 70, 71, 72, 73, 74, 75, 77, 80, 84
Mazalem courts, 17
Means of production, 27, 29
Medinah, 6, 16, 39, 40, 41, 42, 43, 44, 49, 52, 59, 68, 87, 117; Islamic state of, 39, 41, 117; Muslim community in, 87; political groups in, 42
Mehdi, Imam, 10, 12, 111, 115, 117, 129, 131
Messiah, 115, 117
Messianic, 115, 117
Messianism, 115, 116, 129; Islamic, 12, 115, 116, 117, 129, judaeo-Christian idea of, 115
Middle East, 20
Military, 17, 60, 61, 69, 70, 72, 77, 78; administration, 17; defacto authority of, 66; force, 72; leaders, 72; rulers, 69; Turkish, 72
al-Minhaj, 60
Minorities, 48
Mizan (scale), 127
Modernization theories, 20
Modernization theorists, 21
Moghul, 16
Monarchical rule, 9, 59, 72
Monarchy, 40, 44, 45, 112; Perian, 112
Mongol(s), 45, 103, 108
Mosque, 80
Moussavi, Ahmad, 10, 11, 13, 97
Mu'adh ibn Jabal, 81
Mu'awiyah, 44, 65, 72, 110
Muhaddithun (traditionists), 99
Muhajireen, 34, 42, 47
Muhaqqiq-i Hilli, 103, 109
Muhtasib (censor), 17
Mujtahid (independent legal interpreter), 10, 11, 78, 97, 99, 101, 102, 103, 104
Mukallaf(s) (committed Muslims), 99, 100, 104, 105, 110
Mulla(s), 112